SPIRIT
HEALING

SPIRIT
HEALING

HOW TO MAKE
YOUR LIFE WORK

Mary Dean Atwood, Ph. D.

Sterling Publishing Co., Inc.
New York

Edited by Cassia B. Farkas
Book design by Liz Trovato

Library of Congress Cataloging-in-Publication Data Available

2   4   6   8   10   9   7   5   3   1

Published in 2006 by Sterling Publishing Co., Inc.
387 Park Avenue South, New York, NY 10016
© 2004 by Sterling Publishing Co., Inc.
Material in this book was adapted from:
Spirit Herbs, Native American Healing,
© 1998 by Mary Dean Atwood
Spirit Healing, Native American Magic & Medicine,
© 1991 by Mary Dean Atwood;
Distributed in Canada by Sterling Publishing
^{c}/o Canadian Manda Group, 165 Dufferin Street,
Toronto, Ontario, Canada M6K 3H6
Distributed in the United Kingdom by GMC Distribution Services,
Castle Place, 166 High Street, Lewes, East Sussex, England BN7 1XU
Distributed in Australia by Capricorn Link (Australia) Pty. Ltd.
P.O. Box 704, Windsor, NSW 2756, Australia

Sterling ISBN-13: 978-1-4027-4110-4
ISBN-10: 1-4027-4110-3

For information about custom editions, special sales, premium and
corporate purchases, please contact Sterling Special Sales
Department at 800-805-5489 or specialsales@sterlingpub.com.

CONTENTS

Chapter Seven

MEDICINE

 INTRODUCTION

Inspiration to write this came from the hologram of my existence, and includes research findings, personal experiences, observations, teachings from Native Americans, and institutional data derived from my own experiences as a contemporary medicine woman. The list is incomplete unless mention is made of knowledge given from sources not easily named as they come from other planes of existence.

When European settlers arrived on the continent of North America, they found Native Americans healthy and robust. Smallpox, tuberculosis, bubonic plague, syphilis, and other horrible diseases were unknown to their tribes. Early white settlers believed bathing abominable and used no soap. They considered native customs, such as bathing, sweating, and fasting, barbaric.

For centuries, religious settlers were frightened by the animal totems, chanting, rattling of charms, burning of herbs, and use of song and prayer to cure illness. The pilgrims and those who followed had little knowledge of the strange plants and environment they encountered here, and any who showed too much interest in learning from the natives risked persecution for witchcraft.

Native American medicine healers were actually advanced in their holistic approach to healing. Methods used included assessment of personal problems, family or tribal intervention, and dream interpretation to uncover hidden needs and fears. Shamans burned sacred herbs, called for help from powerful spirit guides, and dispensed necessary energy through their hands, totems, or prayers. For serious physical problems or community conflicts, the whole family or tribe gathered together to be included in the healing process. Secret medicine societies of respected elders met together to solve problems affecting the tribe.

In addition to physical illness or damage by accidents or battles, healers recognized the potential dangers of unconscious or unexpressed wishes and needs; that when anger or negative energy forces attacked a tribal member it could cause illness. Medicine healers looked into the unseen

world of the body—the thoughts or dreams of the patient—to deduce the cause of sickness. There the offending spirit or personal problem was located. Sometimes the medicine man or woman left Earth and traveled to the land of the ancestors to obtain necessary information. Their prophecies, often for the benefit of the tribe, came from powerful guides.

Such concerns disconcerted white settlers, because they made little connection between the mind and the health of the body. Unfortunately, in many modern health clinics, *mental state and environment are still ignored!* One might ask which medicine, old or new, is the most primitive?

Lack of knowledge of chemical properties of herbs didn't lessen the medicine man or woman's effectiveness. If a plant or object appeared to cause pleasant or healing events, it was good medicine. If a plant or totem had medicine, it had power. Trial and error undoubtedly contributed to the acquired knowledge. Modern analyses of the chemical composition of plants document the healing qualities of herbs used by the Indians. Today, natural herbal and synthetic duplication of compounds account for numerous over-the-counter and prescription medicines.

What treasures of medicine may not be expected from a people, who although destitute of the lights of science, have discovered the properties of some of the most inestimable medicines.—Dr. Benjamin Barton 1798[1]

A drunken man who had fallen into a fire was burnt in such a manner.... I did not think he could recover; yet they cured him in ten Days, so that he went about. I knew another blown up with Powder that was cured to Admiration. I never saw an Indian have an Ulcer, or foul Wound in my life; neither is there any such thing to be found among them.—John Lawson 1714[2]

Now, five centuries after the pilgrims' arrival, research studies reveal

that more people seek alternative health practitioners using natural remedies, holistic approaches, or spiritual methods than visit standard medical doctors. The percentage continues to grow as awareness increases about healing from the use of nature's bounty and energies not always explained by known physical laws.

We wish to know more about the ways of the medicine men and women who recognized these forces. As the Grandmothers and Grandfathers watch us from the Path of Souls, they, no doubt, are pleased with the wonders of modern medical science. Perhaps they wish for a combined joint effort of old and new to heal ourselves and our planet. We only hope the Native American ancestors who guide our knowledge and wisdom show us the patience and honor not accorded them.

In my attempt to capture the sacred nature of Native American philosophy, so rich in spirit and soul, an overlap will be noted with other religions or ways of life. Native Americans, not unlike followers of Eastern religions, believed that all animal, mineral, and plant life contained a spiritual essence or living force. Current research on DNA in modern Native Americans suggests that North and South American Indians came from one culture in Asia that migrated across the Bering Strait. This could explain similarities between the Eastern religious philosophies and those of the Native Americans, both of which stress the importance of human soul growth as the reason for existence, and the divine spark as an energy shared by other forms in nature. To destroy the other life forms on the planet is to invite your own destruction.

The recent necessity for planetary and wildlife ecology has brought this ancient wisdom to the attention of Western thinking. Our divine energy is connected to the energy of other forms of life. This wisdom, intuitively perceived by Native Americans, will become more obvious as humans cope with the destruction that they have brought to the planet.

The best documentation of the existence of spiritual helpers and life after death has come from the testimonies of survivors of near-death experiences. Interestingly, a shaman typically has such an experience

before he or she receives power. One of my Native American teachers met with the Owl Woman who lives on a star during his near-death experience. He was told that he had to return to earth because he had not done what he needed to do. Numbers of people, including myself, have been privileged to see, hear, or feel other dimensions through vision quests or spirit communications.

Proof is important for the Western mind. As the veil continues to thin between the concrete physical world and the esoteric spirit world, more evidence will be forthcoming for the disbelievers.

The notion of spirit teachers inhabiting another world, such as the Grandmothers and the Grandfathers, is accepted by the oldest religions of the world. Native Americans had relatives from the animal, natural, celestial, and human kingdoms, who often switched from one form to another as they desired, or as lessons were accomplished. Restrictions of time and space were not recognized, although there seem not to have been any specific theories of transmigration.

Some of the exercises in this book were channeled by Native American spirits. This is not a new phenomenon. The reason that many spirit guides have an Indian identity is because the Native Americans had a way of perceiving and living life in a circular as opposed to linear way, which kept them closer to divine power.

Defining "real" Native American practices turned out to be as difficult as trying to prove who are bona-fide Native Americans. In my research, I found that customs and beliefs vary from tribe to tribe. For example, the colors representing each of the four directions were different, but usually chosen from white, black, red, blue, or yellow. For this reason, it goes without saying that any reference to certain ways of doing rituals is only a guide and never the only way to do it.

Problems with genuine Indian traditions begin when one takes into account the tremendous efforts to which mainstream American culture has gone to eradicate all Indian religious practices. The missionaries, worried about saving the souls of Native Americans, successfully altered

traditional ways over the centuries in which they worked with the Indians. The government did the same, but for other reasons. The Native Americans were forbidden to practice their ancient ways and dances because of fears of uprisings. Several hundred men, women, and children were killed at Wounded Knee when an attempt was made to have a Ghost Dance in 1890.

Native Americans have the freedom to conceptualize religion in individual ways, and they do so. Beliefs of my different full-blood Native American teachers vary widely. One expressed sadness that the younger generation does not say its daily prayers facing the sun as she was brought up to do. However, when I asked if the sun was an entity or spirit to which the prayer paid homage, she seemed offended, saying that the prayer was to Jesus alone. This dear Native American, who embodies all that is pure and spiritual in thought and deed, was born in a teepee on a reservation in South Dakota, two decades after the incident at Wounded Knee.

Before the introduction of Christianity, spiritual deities were viewed as having power over the universe, but not being always available for assistance. The lesser animal and nature spirits were sought as practical helpers necessary for one's wellbeing. The notion of one god, such as the Great White Father, is thought by some anthropologists to have resulted after the introduction of Christianity. However, most Native Americans believe that their religion acknowledged the existence of the one Great Spirit thousands of years before white men set foot on their soil. The Eastern religions, which there is evidence they may have shared at one time, profess the great all-knowing, all-powerful force within the universe.

It is westerners who interpreted the many sacred forms within that power as separate deities, instead of viewing them as different representations of a single energy. The various beings and spirits are manifestations of "one" power. Because of that single sacred energy, Native Americans had little difficulty incorporating Jesus into their religious

structure. Westerners, however, felt differently when asked to accept another's spiritual figures.

Most of my Native American teachers were brought up in various Western theologies, and they incorporated those traditions into their own religious practices. Others, such as the lady mentioned on page 13, have had their original religious views eradicated. The majority have a mixed spiritual ideology.

My own interest in Native American traditions began with a series of experiences with bird and animal life that could be defined only in a Native American spiritual framework. I began to be aware that messages were being given to me by my bird and animal brothers and sisters, who could be defined as spirit helpers. There were no books or research on American Indians to describe this phenomenon. Fortunately, my attempt to understand what was happening increased my spiritual experiences. Usually one is guided when one asks to be led. The "knowing" does not come from knowledge, but from "inner wisdom."

Powerful medicine people do not give their information away. Prophetic and healing talents are only given to those individuals who have proven that they have no interest in misusing them. Many of the talents of medicine men and women are natural or earned powers that cannot be taught to others. Secrets that can be shared are given to select people with the right character and dedication for years of study. As the old saying goes, when the pupil is ready, the teacher appears.

The great secret ancient wisdoms come to those who work on their character first. The knowing is acquired when one has lifted one's self to a high enough plane to receive. Few secrets exist on these higher planes of existence and little appears to happen by chance. Sometimes one needs a way to begin a quest for increased knowledge, self healing, and discovery. My hope is that this book will help you begin your journey. Ho!

–Mary Dean Atwood, Ph.D.

Chapter One

MIND

The forefathers of the United States used ideas from the Iroquois Federation when they wrote the Declaration of Independence.

> In our every deliberation, we must consider the impact of our decisions on the next seven generations.
>
> —From the *Great Law* of the Iroquois Confederacy

Today in efforts to move toward better personal health and the preservation of our planet, we again seek ancient wisdom. Spiritual and natural healing methods make us eager to blend native ways with new technologies. It is helpful to compare the thought patterns of traditional red men to those of the European colonists if we are to have success combining the old and new ways toward a better future for all.

TRADITIONAL THINKING

RED MAN	WHITE MAN
Holistic healing	Treating symptoms
Earth is sacred	Earth is to use
Time is circular	Time is linear
Time is relative	Time is precise
Community thinking	Individual thinking
Questioning intrusive	Questioning necessary
Spiritual	Religious
Ambition is crass	Ambition is admired
Advice is ill-mannered	Advice is to be given
Earth/creatures sacred	Earth/creatures relative

Children are little adults	Children need guidance
Life is the teacher	Authorities teach
Staring is rude	Staring shows interest
Honor above winning	Winning brings honor
Person valued	Accomplishment valued
Today-oriented	Goal-oriented
Creative ideas within	Creative ideas external
Kinesthetic learner	Visual/or direct learner
Talking depletes energy	Talking gets things done
Actions show character	Actions bring success
Power is an energy	Power is control
Possessions are communal	Possessions are owned

Tradition changes and every person is an individual with his or her own set of values. Today's Americans are a mixture of races, ideas, religions and goals. The strength of all Americans and people around the world lies in their diversity and ability to change as needed. The traditional views, as described above, reflect the Eastern and Western cultures of the world. Although few people today can claim a "full-blood" heritage, meaning ancestors from only one genetic pool or country, Native Americans' DNA is Oriental in origin, since their ancestors crossed over the Bering Strait into the Americas. Caucasian DNA originated in Western Europe.

Only the strongest Native Americans survived the European invasion. Only the hardiest, most aggressive Caucasians, blacks, and Orientals survived to arrive in the Americas. As a group, they form the American prototype known the world over as ambitious, aggressive, intelligent, capable, attractive, emotional and, yes, crass and "uncultured." Survival of our planet demands that we retain the best traditional and contemporary ideas and dismiss those that are truly outdated or destructive. By combining Eastern introspection and Western action, it is possible to heal ourselves, others, and the planet. We start with our own health, branch out (in our own ways) to help those less fortunate, and then think globally.

THE MAGIC OF THOUGHT

One of the best-kept secrets is the power of thought. You create that which you think. Thinking of someone or something actually creates a thought form that is sent out into the atmosphere. This is the secret. Thoughts are matter.

Native Americans realize the power of prayer, for to pray is to put thoughts into words with intensity. This increases the density of the matter that makes up the thought form. This matter in turn attracts particles on the same vibratory level, continuing to build until the object is formed or materialized.

If you think with emotion, thought particles form faster and travel greater distances. Unfortunately, negative vibrations, such as fear and hate, attract and materialize faster because the intensity of emotion strengthens the words or idea. The more emotion in your thought or wish, the more likely it is to materialize. For this reason, peaceful or beautiful wishes and thoughts must be accompanied by sincerity and love to speed them on their way toward formation.

Early settlers and European visitors to America did not realize how religious the Native Americans were. Because their rituals and customs differed, the spirituality of their nature was overlooked. Although time spent in ceremony and prayer differed between tribes, religion and deity communication occupied an important place in each Native American culture. Their traditional spiritual leaders stressed the importance of honor, power, faith, prayer, sharing, and community.

Their priests, shamans, and leaders recognized the power of a humble manner and of dedication to prayer. They sent requests out into the atmosphere for help and guidance. They asked for assistance from their spiritual helpers, knowing that their prayers would be heard and hoping that their requests would be honored. Intensity of emotion and sincerity was always present, along with self-sacrifice and honor.

In many ways, their levels of spirituality exceeded those of other groups. Today, the recognition that humans are all sisters and brothers to

each other and to the other creatures on the planet is gaining widespread acceptance. It is no accident that Native American philosophy and techniques are being sought by those wishing to learn or to receive higher spiritual blessings in their lives.

Many tenets of Native American religions are similar to those of the major religions of the world, especially the Eastern religions. Although philosophies of the afterlife varied from tribe to tribe, the notion of being one with the universe and the acceptance of a great spiritual or vibrational power present in the essence of humans past and present, was found in most Native American religions. Today, many of the spirit guides and angels that help the planet appear in Native American form. It may be only fitting (given the white settlers' treatment of the Native Americans) that many people today who are interested in Native American religious beliefs are of Western European ancestry.

Other religions recognize the importance of thought, both in content and process (what you think, as well as how and why you are thinking it and the accompanying emotion). Some people believe that this is the key to all higher religious experience.

Native Americans have been characterized as circular thinkers, which allows one's spiritual essence to be more effective (being more concerned with living in the present, feeling what is happening around you, and experiencing the *now*). This is the opposite of linear thinking.

Theda Starr, a Pawnee, is a psychologist and healer. She is a natural therapist and profoundly affects others as she works. Her philosophy in healing is "unraveling one's life, and knitting it back together." She works to define the problem, change the defenses, increase understanding, and then to knit it all back together. She says, "Just begin anywhere—it all needs fixing."

Theda Starr believes that thought is prayer. What you think is essentially a prayer, because it releases energy. If more people were aware of this profound idea, they would be more careful about what they think.

Love, honor, patience, charity, faith, wisdom, and power are universally

considered virtues to be cultivated in thought and deed. While most Americans are familiar with the philosophy of positive thinking, few know how to put it into action. But, before you can enact thoughts that become prayers, you must rid yourself of unwanted mental clutter.

⊟ HEAL THE MIND

Thought is energy, and what the mind believes changes the cellular structure of the body. Desire is the fuel that increases the intensity of the mind energy to accomplish the wish. With a mind-set for healing, the immune system receives an extra boost.

Have you ever noticed that you are more likely to be sick after performing a task you didn't want to do? Conversely, you can be tired and join in a strenuous fun activity and end up feeling better than you did before.

Negative energy from either yourself or the environment depresses the immune system and makes it difficult for spiritual, mental, or herbal remedies to work. Using a natural product in combination with a desire to heal the body actually raises the immune capacity of the body, increasing the vibrational and spiritual level of the body at the same time.

Becoming healthier mentally requires a threefold process:
1. Improve your physical health through better habits and nutrition.
2. Establish a mind-set that feels and knows you to be a sacred person; believe in you; picture yourself perfect in mind and body.
3. Be your unique self; bring fun into your life by "following your bliss."

The mental-emotional component is ignored today despite volumes of research demonstrating the importance of mind-set: at least 75 percent of the time, illnesses are related to problems outside the physical realm. All the medicines in the world won't cure a person who has lost the desire to live. What seemed to some to be paganistic rituals by superstitious witch doctors were important healing processes because they gave patients hope that someone cared and was willing to stay with them, and also created trust in the magic of the shaman to perform the cure.

Studies indicate the importance of doctor-client relationships and trust in the caretaker. This factor is recognized today in Indian hospitals where traditional medicine men and women may work together with contemporary doctors. Again, the holistic approach is preferred.

To help heal yourself both physically and mentally, use natural herbal nervines that:
1. Actually assist in healing the nervous system instead of masking symptoms or dulling the brain.
2. Help relax and calm the mind for a better attitude about yourself and your life.

Contemporary society promotes the tension and stress that account for a large percentage of mental and physical problems. With a plethora of wonderful nervines available at health food stores and specialty stores and, increasingly, in drugstores and grocery stores, there is no reason not to try these herbal remedies. Although they are becoming more expensive as demand develops, they are still inexpensive compared to prescription drugs. Experiment with the nerviness singularly and in combination until you find one remedy that fits your body chemistry the best.

Also try also the wonderful flower essences for nervous problems. One example is the Bach Flower Essences sold in health food stores. Experiment for results and write down findings. One of the mistakes people make is taking a remedy, finding relief, going on with their routine, forgetting what helped them the last time they felt that way, and then forgetting to use it later when the problem returns!

Flower essences can be used as often as you like. They aren't drugs. Try different flower essence brands, herbal support, and gem crystal therapies until you find your favorites.

◧ How to Reduce Tension Situations

Medicine healers in tribes used the whole family and neighbors in healing for emotional problems related to interpersonal interactions. Dreams were analyzed when the emotional crisis was intrinsic. Today, if you can't afford therapy and want to improve your situation, take the initiative to discover and make changes within yourself. The following exercise will help you take crucial steps toward having the life you deserve.

List the situations in which you find yourself feeling:

Powerless_____

_____

_____

Unhappy_____

_____

_____

Angry_____

_____

_____

Sad_____

_____

_____

Tense_____

_____

_____

Anxious_____

_____

_____

Embarrassed_____

_____

_____

Inadequate_____

_____

_____

Include situations from your past and present that bring these feelings to memory. Are there recurring themes? Is there a common thread that gives you clues to the reason for the problem? For each situation listed, write them out on paper.

◱ CHECKLIST

1. Are you trying to control other people?

_____

_____

_____

_____

2. Is your pride or ego involved?

_____

_____

_____

_____

3. Are you afraid of being hurt emotionally?

_____

_____

_____

_____

4. Do you avoiding making decisions?

_____

_____

_____

_____

5. Do materialistic concerns take precedence over people?

_____

_____

_____

_____

6. Are you angry or resentful?

_____

_____

_____

_____

7. Do you see everything as black or white?

_____

_____

_____

_____

8. Are you being deceitful or having to lie?

_____

_____

_____

_____

9. Are you jealous or suspicious?

_____

_____

_____

_____

10. Are you doing what you want to do in life?

_____

_____

_____

_____

Check any question that applies to you and list beside it what situations made you feel that way. *Determine the specific life event where you find yourself feeling your worst. Then state the first, most-important single action you must do to correct this negative situation.* Write down the first step you have to take to change from a nervous state to a happier one.

The situation where I feel the worst is

_____

_____

_____

_____

What I must do to take action on this problem is

_____

_____

_____

_____

Changing old negative habits and patterns is difficult, but if you truly want with all your heart to change your life, you must stick to whatever action is needed and follow through regardless of whatever excuses you come up with not to.

After following through on the first, most-important single thing to do, the second step, the action needed to solve the problem, is taken. If you are sincere and truly striving for a better life with no ill intent to others, you will be assisted from higher powers to succeed.

Now that you've attacked your worst stresses, the intent to change your life will begin to transform the physical/mental/spiritual cellular makeup of your body. We possess primordial memory traces in our bodies, cells and genes from the previous experiences of our ancestors and, some believe, our past lives. In addition, the experiences throughout our life impact our current skeletal/muscular and mental/emotional cellular structure.

One important hint to reducing stress is to avoid vacillating about decisions. *Learn to say yes-yes or no-no to every situation and then stick to it.* Give yourself several opportunities to assess the situation, make your decision and stay with it until the situation in which you are "stuck" no longer exists. Do not deviate from your goal to conquer the most important change you need to make in your life. It will happen if you really want to change. Use herbal formulas to assist you and watch the positive changes that will take place in your life. Good luck!

◧ CHANGING THOUGHT PATTERNS

Before changes are made, however, you must first identify the theme or scripts you think about during your day.

1. Set your alarm at different intervals to catch yourself thinking, then record your thoughts on the left side of a piece of paper. Across the page, opposite your thoughts, record the general theme of your thoughts. For example, if you find yourself thinking of paying your phone bill at 1:00 and thinking of finding the money for new shoes at 1:15, both thoughts are different in content but have the same theme—concern about debts or money. You have a preoccupation with financial security.

2. If you are currently dealing with a crisis or problem, then you are aware of where some of your thought energy is going. Although you know where you stand on the subject, you may not be aware of the nature of your thoughts or thought processes or of the specific fears running through your mind. The more fearful or traumatic the situation, the more your unconscious fears and old habits take over. It is necessary that you identify these ruminations before you can successfully change your way of thinking. Use the alarm or write down your repetitive thoughts. What is the theme or underlying concern or fear?

HEALING YOURSELF

The formula for healing yourself is:

STOP—LOOK—LISTEN—TAKE ACTION

Stop! Stop thinking the unwanted thought. Say "stop" to yourself.

Look! Look specifically at what you were thinking.

Listen! Listen for the underlying theme. What are you afraid of? What is the emotion behind the concern? Watch particularly for fear, anger, despair, jealousy, suspicion, resignation, pride, and need for escape. Has there been self-sabotage, carelessness, erratic behavior or laziness in your actions?

Take Action!

    A
    C
    T
    I   (inner faith)
    O (own up to your responsibility in the problem)
    N (now let go)

Take action by saying aloud:

"**I** have faith in myself, my higher self, and my heavenly helpers, to seek out what is best for me."

Own your part in this worry. "I did _____ and this caused _____," or, "I permitted _____ to do _____," or, "**I** chose to be with _____."

Now, let go. "I _____ (your name) let go of worrying about _____. If needed, I will take a specific action, but I will let go of thinking about this."

See and feel this problem, person, or situation floating up into the sky surrounded by white light. Now it is gone. If you find yourself thinking or worrying about this same situation repeat: "_____ (your first name), let go."

Practice getting rid of worries and concerns that keep your mind cluttered with problems. Remember: *Thought is prayer*. When you keep your mind focused on problems, *you bring more of those problems into your life*. You attract the same vibrations that you send out. Change your thoughts or prayers to bring only good things into your life. Repeat the preceding exercise until you change your unconscious thought patterns. Do not be discouraged. Some sages spend their whole lives perfecting their thinking. If you begin to have more dreams of problems, know that your plan is working. For as you rid yourself of fears during the day, your unconscious will attempt to bring them back at night! This will last only for a night or two before your unconscious begins to change its conditioning.

Now that you have obtained some control over your thoughts, you can begin to insert higher thoughts and ideals in your daily thinking.

⊟ MATERIALIZING WHAT YOU WANT

Sai Baba, the great Eastern Indian religious leader, produces articles from his hands through thought. He has materialized hundreds of articles of jewelry, prayer beads, and sacred ash to people all over the world. Drinks Water, the famous Lakota Sioux medicine man, produced articles such as food, tobacco or matches as he needed them just by thinking of them. Helene Blavatsky, author of *The Secret Doctrine*, once materialized a cup and saucer to match her set when she needed one to serve another guest.

While you may not achieve these feats of materialization, you can accomplish even more important ones, such as changing the events that will occur in your life. Start now. By dwelling on several important ideals or emotions, you can begin to attract these qualities to you. Once you have weeded out many undesirable worries, fill that space with thoughts and

ideals that can change your life. Bring love, protection, opportunity, goals, blessings for others, and needed goods into your life by thinking of them.

☐ SELF-IMPROVEMENT

Analyze the qualities you most need or wish to cultivate and list them in order of preference. Start with your weakest quality. Then take this quality and think the word whenever you eat or drink during the day. For example, let's say you have the most trouble enjoying yourself. Think *joy* while you take a bite of food or drink something. Also, feel *joy* while you think it. This will help insert this quality into your subconscious and also attract it to you. Think this quality during the day, as the last thing before you go to sleep, and during the first five minutes after awakening.

Analyze the negative qualities most often present in your thoughts or behavior. Keep in mind the list above under *listen*. Select one negative attribute. Once a day, when going to the bathroom or showering (getting rid of unwanted bodily effects), picture this quality leaving your body at the same time. Feel it slough off your body, getting rid of it totally. Imagine it gone. After you have mastered that undesired quality, work on another. Choose the more powerful negative qualities to conquer first.

☐ SUBSTITUTE POSITIVE FOR NEGATIVE

Negative qualities also can be countered with positive ones. For example, if you have a tendency to be depressed, think joy whenever you get a sad feeling.

Stop! When you catch yourself thinking and feeling a negative thought, such as a bad thing that someone did to you, stop.

Look! Now look for and substitute a desirable or needed thought and feeling in the place of the one that you removed, such as forgiveness instead of resentment (feel the substituted thought).

Listen! Now listen to yourself saying the positive word or phrase such as "I forgive _____," (and feel it).

◧ Now You Are Manifesting!

In addition to the positive traits that you wish to acquire, other phrases and wishes may be used as affirmations. Some examples are:

1. Repeat inspirational or religious phrases such as: "In God We Trust. Love Thy Neighbor as Thyself. Glory to God in the Highest. Peace on Earth, Good Will to Men."

2. Substitute a thought or wish for a needed happening or article, such as "Heal _____ (name)" or "Provide money for my _____ (needed article)."

3. Devise personal affirmations such as: "I am getting healthier and healthier," "I make the right decisions," and "I allow myself to receive love."

4. When certain items or situations are needed, be specific in your requests. For example, say "I need patience when I attend the closing next Wednesday." If your whole life seems to be desperate and you wish for divine intervention, make general requests, such as "Thy will be done. I will accept what is best for me," or repeat prayers such as the twenty-third psalm, which begins "The Lord is my shepherd, I shall not want."

◧ Thought Control

The more control you have of your thoughts, the more effective you will be in manifesting what you want from life. The following are some exercises to help you gain more control.

1. Follow your train of thought for ten minutes. Do not analyze your thoughts, or try to focus them in a certain direction. Just follow your mind wherever it goes.

2. Now, try to think of only one thing for ten minutes. Decide what single sentence or thought you want to concentrate on, and do so for ten minutes. Do not let any other thoughts intervene. When they do, push them aside and go on.

3. Now empty your mind for ten minutes. Clear your mind totally. Look at the clock when you begin. At first you only may be able to do this for a minute or two. Keep practicing until you achieve a ten-minute interval.

4. When you can do all of the above exercises, you will be able to achieve lofty spiritual goals and manifest a better life.

⊟ JOY WALK

One of the best ways to practice daily affirmations is to incorporate them into a joy walk. As you enjoy the outdoors and observe nature, you can insert some words or phrases of affirmation. Feel joy as you say them.

After you have enjoyed the silence of the outdoors, begin to chant your new words and phrases of joy. A melody may come to mind. Sing it to yourself if others are around. Put your intense desires and highest spiritual needs to the melody. Time it in rhythm to your step!

Your joy song will differ from your power song as you deliberately will compose the words to become an affirmation for needed development. The power song may have only a few words and is developed from the subconscious.

You will want to sing your joy walk song during your walk, when you are driving, or when you are at home. After the song becomes automatic, your unconscious will be ready to help manifest that which you desire!

Need for Protection Rituals

True medicine healers and today's gifted men and women can see into the fourth dimension, a plane where unseen energies—thought forms, earthbound beings, and angelic helpers—reside. Viewing the invisible world, it is easy to recognize a need to help people protect themselves. Those who know recognize three main forces or entities against which we all need protection.

Leftover vibrations—that still hang around due to undesirable people, activities, or unfriendly ghosts. The clearing rituals described in this and the next chapter can get rid of this type unless something negative brings it back.

Energy vampires—usually needy family members or friends who are quite unaware of their "talent" for draining the life energy from other people. After you have been in contact with them, they feel better, and you feel worse! Spouses, teenagers, needy friends, and sickly relatives are usually the unwitting culprits, as they have no ill intent or awareness of the process.

Drainers—as a phenomenon this is a foreign concept to most modern people, who dismiss it as superstition. However, "rational thinking" in our culture doesn't make the phenomenon go away. Like electricity running through your TV, draining energy can run through your body even though you don't see it. One day this phenomenon will be proven by scientific experiments based on quantum physics.

Drainers are able to draw your energy only because you feel a need to take care of them—either because of guilt, a need for self-punishment, or a desire to keep the person around you. In some cases, it is necessary to assume responsibility for a person, as a parent does for children. Small children need complete care for a long time, but cannot draw energy unless the parent continually fosters it through a wish to be needed.

People need to make appropriate decisions about whom and what they are responsible for, and act accordingly. Because we want to be able to give to and support particular people, we need to learn to protect our-

selves from losing vital strength. Self-protection does not effect your being able to love and take care of these people; it improves your ability to be nurturing because you are not unduly tired and over-extended.

It is interesting that people who lack nurturing skills or have the ability to detach themselves, appropriately or not, seldom have this problem. Some of the worst cases of draining happen to highly spiritual people who have not yet learned to protect themselves, or to average people made vulnerable due to a devastating loss or injury.

Couples, especially those in karmic—or codependent—relationships, are especially adept at drawing energy from each other. Sleeping together is one of the best times for astral traveling, and the physical proximity makes the draining process easier. Remember, most people have no idea this phenomenon is happening. A pull can also occur between people who have never had sex or slept together, if one or both desires the other with intensity. Be careful what you wish for—or as Elizabeth Barrett Browning put it, "God often answers our prayers, a gift with a gauntlet in it."

It is natural that susceptibility to draining increases in times of crisis, usually with one partner doing a better job of collecting energy. Usually drainers end up married or living with martyr-type personalities. Your partner cannot drain your energy unless you need that person as much as he or she needs you.

People with addictions are especially attractive to entities. Earthbounds (ghosts) and bad thought-forms can latch on to them and drain their energy. Because the spirits aren't alive but want to experience their former habits, they try to get a living person to carry out their fantasies, such as drinking, engaging in sexual encounters, or taking drugs. Although greatly overdone by Hollywood (people being taken over by evil spirit entities that make them do things they would never do), it does happen with people in intoxicated or drugged states because they aren't "all there." Their etheric bodies, which surround the physical, are full of holes and are easily penetrated.

Native Americans were right about the existence of undesirable energy fields, such as might be felt in an ancient dungeon where terrible acts occurred. Some ghosts are friendly, either waiting on Earth for their loved ones to join them, or confused and thinking they are still alive. The dangerous ghosts are those whose earthly behavior resulted in such low vibrational states they couldn't ascend to a higher level.

Occasionally a spirit may just like it here. A famous, drug-addicted singer who is frequently sighted alive may be roaming around with a spirit body dense enough to be seen by people with "the sight." Sensitives can see thought-form energies, such as a bright aura, or negative energies, which are dark and jagged. Mediums can sometimes see images of people who have just left the room.

The most important protection and clearing ritual you can do for yourself is to let go of your own habits, addictions, and dependencies. Next, rid or detach yourself from negative people, places, and things. *The worst enemy or negativity around us is the third form: our own thought-forms.* They have occurred so often in our minds that the energy occupies a dense space (think of it as a dark cloud) that hangs around the head and body all the time.

These thoughts, of course, are the hardest to get rid of because we tend to rerun old mental tapes over and over in our heads. To clairvoyants, seeing these energies around a person is like looking at Medusa with the snakes coming out of her head! You can smoke a room from the inside; give away clothes, jewelry, and furniture to get rid of vibrations; avoid bad energy scenes such as seedy or low-life locations; or choose to try another spouse, but you are still stuck with your own imagination and mind.

Ninety percent of imagined enemies, ghosts, persecution complexes, and paranoid states are created in our own minds, and people with these serious problems may suffer their whole lifetimes with such afflictions. The rest of us go in and out of this state as natural changes and life's problems test us over and over again. Although not widely recognized in our society, the lunar cycle and the rotation of planets has considerable impact on our states of mind.

FINDING YOUR POWER TOTEM

Olympic winners, medicine healers, politicians, and metaphysical people share one thing in common: They often believe in an object, or "totem," they carry with them to help assure success when competing, healing, or needing assistance. Believing in a totem "helper" gives them the self-confidence that makes the difference between success and failure.

The traditional red man uses objects of nature. An Olympic champion might wear the same pair of socks in each competition. A priest will wear a Christian cross. A politician uses campaign buttons and slogans as a power affirmation. Single, dating adults hope a special cologne or style of dress will enhance their desirability.

A totem can be any object, hobby, interest, slogan, picture, scent, plant, animal, stone, thought, role model, or song. It should be a positive thought reminder that actually makes you feel good about yourself, increases self-confidence, and empowers you. Ideas for finding one will be offered. You don't need more than one but can have as many as you want—provided you focus on a single quality you want to cultivate.

◧ MAGIC INVENTORY

An object or idea for a totem to be your lucky charm is around you. Pretend you are an observing stranger in your surroundings. What indications are present?

1. Do you notice a large number of pictures or art with one theme or subject matter that suggests a totem? An example might be a collection of books or artwork on one subject.

2. Do you have a special hobby or collect ceramic animal statues or other types of figurines?

3. Is there a list of dates for events or activities you wanted to do but never took the time? What do they have in common?

4. Have you purchased information on planting or growing particular flowers or herbs? Do you like certain tastes and smells that remind you of pleasant foods or experiences such as hiking or camping?

5. Is there a certain book you've wanted to read on self-improvement or a better quality of life? Are you intrigued by a particular religion or practice, such as meditation or yoga, or a representative artifact?

6. A totem can also be a religious figure from your spiritual belief system, such as Jesus or Buddha. It can be a symbol such as a cross, which is widely used as a source of strength and comfort.

7. Have you bought or inherited a special piece of jewelry? Do you have a rock collection (remember, stones have vibrations)?

8. Did someone recently give you a gift that might have special significance, such as a tie or belt with an emblem on it? Do the clothes in your closet have the same color as decorative items in your home?

9. Have you joined an association or studied a particular animal or bird or been interested in the preservation of our planet? This could be an important clue to a certain totem.

10. Do you have an interest in astrology or astronomy? Do you have shapes of moons, stars, the sun, or other sun sign emblems (such as fish for the sun sign Pisces) decorating your home?

Look around your house for an object or idea that might be your totem or lucky charm. Unconsciously, we often have an affinity for items or know what will help us to get in touch with our innermost feelings. Search for the object or an information source to find it, and begin immediately to use it. Associate the article with power and self-confidence.

If you can't find any clues, visiting your favorite hobby store or reading books can help you. The right book frequently appears at a time we

need the help it offers; sometimes a person just happens to bring by a gift at a seemingly coincidental time.

If your lucky charm does not bring you results or renewed confidence, put it away and look again. If you sincerely want your power totem, it will appear in an amazingly timely fashion.

Look for repetitions. One person discovered turtle artifacts all over the house—tape holders, incense burners, jewelry designs and boxes, and stone statues made of jade and soapstone—combined with a habit of rescuing tortoises and turtles on the highways! All of this when no awareness that any interest in the ancient reptiles existed!

◧ CARE AND FEEDING OF YOUR TOTEM

First, you must believe in the totem for it to work. Faith brings joy and optimism, which in turn raises your level of vibrations to a stronger (or higher), more accessible level. The unseen world of angels and spirit guides (or laws of quantum physics if you prefer) operates along powerful energy lines determined by forces we currently are only beginning to discover scientifically. Spiritual people believe a thought is a prayer and what you think is what you create. This is the secret behind why a totem works.

Research has shown that the presence of an experimenter and the way the equipment is arranged may affect the outcome of the data. Atomic particles so tiny that they cannot be seen under the most powerful microscope can be measured only by the trails they leave behind. Scientific experiments show tiny particles not only have a strange way of behaving the way the experimenter desires but also appear to have a choice whether they are going to act like a wave or a particle!

Research shows that smiling, even when you don't feel like it, actually begins to change blood chemistry and improves the immune system! The increase in your optimism and the consequent higher vibrations are then absorbed by your totem and other items around you. These embedded vibrations are why psychics can pick up information from holding a person's ring or article of clothing. Their existence is also a good reason to avoid old objects that have a history of bad luck.

Other practices you can adopt to increase the power of your totem:

1. Keep it wrapped in natural cloth in an accessible but secure place away from the touch of other people, such as in a drawer.

2. Wear or hide it in a pocket or purse when you go to church, attend spiritual meetings or uplifting concerts, get together with friendly people, or visit beautiful places in nature. Doing so encodes higher vibrational levels in yourself and your totem.

3. Use the subject matter or nature of the object to enhance your self-confidence and positive thinking. For example, concentrate on the help received from your totem when you touch, see, or think of it.

4. The single most important emotional state and powerful single word to obtain personal dominion (power) is *joy*. The state of joy, bliss, samadha, in whatever language, heals body, mind, and soul. If you could maintain the emotional state of joy, you would obtain everything in the world you ever wanted with little effort.

Unfortunately, human beings have memory banks of fear and primitive survival defenses that make joy almost impossible to maintain. But—whenever and however you do it—it helps cancel out the thousands of negative messages we give ourselves daily! Faith in yourself and a higher power will help you obtain inner peace.

There are no easy guidelines and clear directions for changing unconscious patterns. At times, we are at the mercy of our own weaknesses, terrors, and self-defeating behaviors. They control our behavior more than is generally admitted. Typically, our behaviors consist of 90 to 95 percent automatic, unconscious habits. To break undesired or ineffectual behavior, absolute determination and steady persistence are required.

When you assume responsibility for yourself and your life, you claim your right to have power and happiness. Thought is energy, and what

the mind believes changes the cellular structure of the body. Desire increases the intensity of the mind energy to actually manifest these wishes in people's lives.

⊞ DAILY TOTEM POWER RITUALS

Increase positive daily habits and automatic behaviors to combat unconscious or fearful self-defeating behaviors. Double or triple your self-improvement by doing numerous faith and power totems during the day. Adopt these suggestions or create your own:

Morning: Stick your lucky totem or totem symbol in your pocket if you are leaving the house. If staying home, place your totem where you will notice it during the day. If you have totem jewelry, be sure to wear it (inside your clothes if you don't want it seen). Use a special scent if relevant. Carry your special book or picture with you if it is your totem.

Daily: Always have a representative reminder of your totem at home, in your workplace, and in your car if possible. Don't tell anyone of its meaning for you. If appropriate, place a symbol of the totem on the telephone, your billfold, the bathroom mirror, or some other frequently used item.

Before Bedtime: Sniff your selection of aromatherapy remedies or favorite scent. Sleep with a totem by your bedside or read inspirational books or articles. Note: Do not watch or read horror stories with bizarre, discouraging or brutal themes; they will stay in your unconscious all night.

Instead, go to sleep with a repetitive positive affirmation tape you have purchased or made yourself. Avoid tapes with subliminal messages unless you know what you will hear. Be sure there are no negative statements because the unconscious only hears the action word. For example, don't tell your children, "Don't forget to feed the dog!" The correct suggestion is, "Remember to feed the dog!"

All the Time: Place a lucky coin, small green stone, or tiny totem in your purse or wallet to remind you of your power and prosperity.

◨ Claiming Your Own Power

Claiming your right to be happy and have dominion (power) doesn't mean you hurt or rule over other people. It means you claim your right as a spiritual person to live a fulfilled life, to experience joy, to have positive relationships, and to develop your own unique talents and skills.

Those of us living in countries not at war or experiencing famine, where survival skills take precedence over personal fulfillment, may have the luxury of working on personal evolution and self-improvement. Working on transformation and growth of the soul can be difficult and scary as change usually brings on anxiety. Giving up old habits requires immense effort.

All the herbs and medicines won't cure you if you don't want to get well or you have self-defeating behaviors and thoughts that make you sick. This is the central meaning of this chapter, which deals with the "medicine" or power base for healing. Mind and body work together.

HOW TO HAVE A VISION

One of the seemingly magical gifts a medicine man or woman demonstrated was predicting the future. This is a gift now available to many people.

Your "sixth sense" or unconscious knows exactly what will happen in a certain situation if you allow that message to come through. However, magical gifts of prophecy disappear or come back to harm you (what goes around comes around) if used in a manipulative or selfish way. For this reason, only people desiring or having done personal growth work are handed this gift.

At first, the ability to divine is treacherous at best because people tend to see and hear what satisfies their wishes. If you get messages or see visions that are too good to be true, they probably are.

Experimenting with trying to improve your clairvoyant skills is a fascinating hobby that can do nothing but improve your life even when you are wrong. Errors point out where you went wrong and what interfered with the correct perception. "Knowing" what will happen doesn't prevent the occurrence if it is a karmic lesson, but you will be better prepared to handle the event. The "gift of sight" is only given to those who will not use the information for self-promotion. Information from a channel for a spiritual voice will not give you material that would change your soul's journey.

Non-ethical or uninformed psychics can give you incorrect data that is destructive to your welfare. Even the best psychics, when they are "on," are only accurate eighty-five to ninety percent of the time. Receiving money, doing too many readings, and knowing the client personally are all dangers to an accurate reading because the psychic is personally involved with and wanting to please the client. Think about how much you want your own heartfelt desires!

With these warnings in mind, now let's work on becoming a visionary. Be sure to light a sacred herb or incense before you begin. Aromas trigger unconscious memories and feelings in the brain which help bring needed material to the surface. If desired, drink some herbal tea made from the "nerve herbs" listed in chapter four. Use tea bags or tincture or take capsules of the nervine with a warm drink.

1. Sit down alone in a quiet place with *no direct question or request on your mind*. Ask only for guidance from a higher power or your higher self. Have a pencil and a piece of paper with you.

2. Do whatever it takes to blank out your mind as much as possible, knowing thoughts will come in and out of consciousness.

3. Sitting quietly by yourself whether taking a bath, smoking a pipe, listening to "white noise" such as a fan, petting your dog, or just resting in the woods or on your own porch are examples of activities which allow the left brain or logical mind-set to temporarily slow down. The right-brain begins to intuit and naturally create. Put all active problem-solving thinking as far away as possible. If you have trouble clearing your mind, meditate, take a bath or lie down, playing soothing music before beginning.

4. Now, while watching your fishing line, sitting by a tree, or feeling the top of your dog's head, try to have a "no-brainer" as you do your relaxed activities. Later, when you find yourself thinking, write down the thought. Repeat the clearing of your mind and then writing down what you find yourself thinking next.

Now you have your WHAT, a topic in which you are currently in need of help. It doesn't matter if it seems unimportant or is nonsensical; it may be a symbol of an important issue.

5. Now, regardless of where you are or what you are doing, look around again, totally uninterested in the result. What do you see around you? Look to the clouds and see if you see a picture in them. If you are around water, watch for pictures in the waves or in the sand. If you are around birds, notice what kind you see and what they are doing

with each other.[3] If you are sitting on your deck, look for emblems or pictures in the wood. If you are inside your home, glance at familiar paintings, statues or figurines to see if you see something in them you hadn't noticed before. If your eyes are closed, be aware of any thoughts or events that pop into your mind. *Your unconscious, or sixth sense, will present you with information* much like a Rorschach blot on a personality test. You will see something new, have a thought, or "know" or feel an emotion. This is HOW this situation will turn out.

6. Be aware that each person has his or her personal "open window" or means for using psychic abilities. With practice, some people can shut their eyes and see pictures, while others feel or sense information. People with psychic talent often prefer to use playing or tarot cards, read palms, or gaze into an object like a crystal. The unconscious sees in these objects something of importance. Experiment with your psychic talent because it may be entirely different in method from others.

7. After your experience, write your results in a notebook. What was the problem and what was the single most important thought or discovery you were given to solve the problem?

8. Dreaming will often answer a question or tell you of an approaching problem. Start a dream notebook in which you record yours. Dreaming of events is often prophetic of events which will occur in the next several days to usually no more than six weeks. A life-changing event may be forecast six months ahead. For dreaming solutions to a problem, ask yourself before you go to sleep to dream the answer to a problem.

When discovering information, if you find fears and or tears arise, stay with the feelings and let them surface. Concentrate on expressing them: don't try to cover up or suppress your emotions. This will be the most important step in working out your solutions. Before new and better

experiences in your life emerge, it is necessary and often painful to clear away the feeling blocking your progress. Remember, energy can't be destroyed, it only changes form. Repressing or suppressing anger, fear, guilt, or grief doesn't get rid of these feelings; they only seek expression in more unconscious and destructive ways.

After allowing these emotions to surface, you can work through them and then continue progressing in your life toward bigger and better things. Often, in order to make opportunities in life or alter negative behavior patterns, a drastic change is needed in yourself. Don't think changing someone else is going to do it for you. It won't. If a pattern in your life is destructive, you are the common denominator. If you keep doing what you have always done, you are going to get what you've always gotten. Ask for guidance and you will get it.

Chapter Two

PLACE

The easiest way to learn to tune into positive energy fields is by visiting religious spots, shrines, and ancient places of worship. This will give you a chance to experience the vibrations of true power locations, because their power is contained or condensed, and therefore strong. Churches, such as the Santuario of Chamayo in New Mexico, emanate sacred energy, which you will feel as soon as you enter. Larger power areas have "hot spots" that generate powerful positive vibrations, but you must seek them out and they are harder to feel.

Once you know what a positive, powerful energy field feels like, you can begin to locate your own in unknown areas. To experience energy, you must take the time to clear your mind and tune in to your body as it receives the waves that are invisible but present. It may make you dizzy, like you are being gently pushed or disoriented as your body adjusts to the strong, spiritual essence. Waves of power may be experienced on your face. You will feel well, rejuvenated, and at peace. Once you know the feeling, you can explore areas close to your home and find your own place of power!

FINDING YOUR POWER PLACE

Explore surrounding areas to find a location where you can sit and reflect or meditate. It may not be necessary to travel long distances. Neighborhood parks contain some surprising places for meditation. The key ingredient is foliage. You must have an area where you can have privacy without prying eyes or excess noise. If you are lucky, a spiritual energy or force will be present in your secluded spot. It may be necessary to travel further. National forests, lakes, river banks, and mountains all

provide countless areas isolated enough for reflection and thought, often with powerful positive energies.

Finding true power centers or sacred locations is more difficult. Mountains act as antenna and certain points or crevices are funnels for magnetic fields. Mount Sinai, Machu Picchu, and the Himalayas are world renowned as strong, sacred energy centers. But pilgrimages to these areas are costly and difficult for westerners and are usually once-in-a-lifetime journeys.

Natural springs and caverns are frequently good sites for spiritual renewal. Energy from the earth emanates from these holes in the ground, drawing to them spirit life and human life alike. Waterfalls and hot springs are naturally cleansing because of the presence of ozone and negative ions in the air.

Trees also have positive energies, as do some natural rocks and plants. The pine and oak tree both vibrate on high spiritual frequencies. Trees are healers and to sit among them invites physical rejuvenation and spiritual renewal. To sit with your back to them or to hug them will facilitate healing in the body. Forests, such as those in the Great Rocky Mountains, are popular locations for quests and for exploring.

Boulders also have desirable magnetic qualities. This is why locations such as the Garden of the Gods in Colorado Springs attract thousands of people a year. It is no accident that some Native American ruins are located in cliffs. When visiting them, you can feel the power emanating from the ancient ceremonial kivas, as you look down over them.

Some power places are sacred because they are holy areas on Mother Earth's body. Other power centers are homes for the spirits that supervise the evolution of mineral, plant, and animal life. Shamans believe the great energy centers are inhabited by great spirits and occasionally visited by the Great Creator. Holy places must be visited always with reverence and respect. This is why the Native Americans observed certain cleansing procedures before and during their visits.

Historical power centers like Spiro National Monument in Oklahoma,

Snake Mound in Ohio, Stonehenge in England, the Big Sur area in California, Chaco Canyon in New Mexico, and the mountains around Sedona, Arizona are sacred places, whether people who visit know it or not. It is dangerous to desecrate holy places.

Occasionally, an area will have bad vibrations due to certain ley lines or habitation by lower forms of spirit. Humans with evil pasts are often stuck on earth, sometimes unable to transcend into the high spiritual planes for centuries, until karmic resolution has occurred. I have found these spirits to be most prevalent around old watering holes, underground springs, or scenes of murder or violent death, as well as areas where humans have violated nature's laws. Sometimes lower forms occupy an area where the earth's negative ley lines intersect. Unfortunately, homes sometimes are located on top of them. Never stay in any location where you experience discomfort or countless problems.

Clearing Herbs

Native Americans used smudging herbs to remove bad energy fields around people. Clearing herbs, offered to Plant Spirits, possessed special powers in getting rid of unseen, troublesome entities such as ghosts or displeased beings. Smudging herbs cleansed the doctor and patient and attracted spirit helpers. This ancient ritual is still practiced today by traditional Native Americans and by anyone else who wants to purify himself or his surroundings of supernatural or malefic influences.

Smudging or clearing herbs are used to clear undesirable vibrations out of homes and off people and to promote health. People and places have a certain feeling or energy. People leave traces of their personalities in their homes. Entering someone's home may make you feel uplifted and vibrant. A home or property might cause an uncomfortable feeling or have a musty odor or cold spot. Real-estate agents comment on the vibrations of a house as due to the energies of previous occupants.

The uncomfortable feeling you can get when entering certain houses need not be caused by a ghost, although "sensitives" believe that ghosts do leave a certain presence in a home. Because children and animals have not developed "rational thinking," they sense these vibrations more easily than adults do.

It is well-known that the moods of someone with whom you are living affect your behavior and emotional state. Everyone has been around a *drainer*, or person who saps your energy. Susceptible people, usually loved ones, end up exhausted. Native Americans, especially the healers, used burning herbs and woods to help remove unwanted energies and restore strength and power.

Instructions for using cleaning and smudging herbs are given in this chapter. People wanting to improve their lives will experiment and draw their own conclusions. But before discussing specific methods, it is useful to look at the Indians' awareness of unseen energy fields. Anthropological psychologists think that belief in the prominence of destructive forces in the Native American environment increased greatly after the Indian way of living was interrupted by white Europeans.

Indigenous peoples believed illness, even accidents, resulted primarily from unseen forces. Negative energies in a person or the environment wreaked havoc and destruction and required dream analysis or family therapy. Shamans could solve individual and clan problems, but the dreaded illnesses resulting from spells or curses from invisible beings such as ghosts or angry spirit entities terrified even the bravest and strongest warrior.

Thus, ceremonial customs accompanying herb use played a large role in contacting and attracting beneficial plant spirits or powerful beings to help eliminate undesirable energy forces. Smoking or smudging herbs and plants purified the air and removed physical problems and malignant energies.

◧ NATIVE AMERICAN CLEARING HERBS

Native Americans, living in the open, didn't have to worry about not getting enough fresh air or breathing too much smoke. Their active lives centered around working and living in the out-of-doors. They weren't polluted from chemicals and city-living smoke and fumes. Clearing herbs, like all burning substances, should be used for specific reasons and in moderation.

Among the most popular purifying herbs and plants were cedar, juniper, sage, sweet grass, pinon, red willow, and mesquite: aromatic scents that pleased the senses and the spirits. Especially appealing to nature beings were herbs prized for their aroma and smoke, which ballooned into giant puffs enveloping large areas when burned. Billowing smoke from these plants rose to greet the spirit messengers.

Herbs used for inhaling or burning smoke for pleasure, ceremony, or respiratory illnesses were angelica, bearberry, coltsfoot, deer's tongue, mullein, yerba santa, sumac leaves, dogwood, corn silk, and valerian,[4] as well as tree barks such as laurel, squaw bush, maple bush, cherry, poplar, birch, wood betony, rose, and arrowwood.

◧ SMUDGING TODAY

Today's contemporary shaman may use Eastern Indian incense such as sandalwood, myrrh, or frankincense. Incense can be purchased in myriad scents. To assure a quality product, try to identify companies located in the region where the natural plant is grown. For example, purchase pinon processed in New Mexico or other southwestern states. Eastern incense, such as myrrh, is best obtained from companies located in India or Far Eastern countries and is readily available in America.

Aromatic herbs and plants can be purchased loose or pressed. After drying, the herbs or barks are sold loose, powdered, or bundled (to make a smudge stick). Smudging plants or substances from them can be compressed to form smudging bundles, incense sticks, or small cones.

Pressed cones of pinon and mesquite contain delightful aromas. To light these, hold the larger bottom of the cone with one hand while you light the pointed end of the cone with the other. After it begins to flame brightly, blow out the fire but continue to blow on the cone to keep it smoldering. Then set the cone in a fireproof container so the sides are not touching anything that would stop the burning process.

For loose or powdered herbs, charcoal is frequently used to facilitate smoldering. Continue to baste the charcoal from time to time with herbs or their powder or oil. Flat charcoal cakes, available in religious and metaphysical stores, light easily so herbs can be placed on top. Plants and incense samples can be tested for personal preferences and comfort as well as effectiveness of results.

Large brush-sage smudging bundles should never be burned in the house around carpet or flammable objects, as sparks create a fire hazard. Even when you think you're being careful, invariably you end up with holes in the carpet. When using smudging herbs indoors, keep them in a large fireproof container and do not leave any smoldering herbs unattended.

For effectiveness, safety, aroma, ease, length of burning time, and availability, it is difficult to surpass incense sticks burned in an incense holder. Indoors these are wonderful for meditation and ceremonies, especially when you do not want to stop to replenish supplies.

Using herbs outside is a different story. Use your campfire or ceremonial fire to burn woods such as pinon, mesquite, cedar, or brush sage. Never cut down healthy trees; look for damaged shrubs, sticks, or dead wood. Green wood doesn't burn and you contribute to the preservation of greenery on our planet when you respect trees.

There is no substitute for participating in a spiritual adventure in the wild. Today, supervised sweat lodges, rope courses, nature hikes, or camping enrich peoples' lives. Observing nature together or by yourself on a vision quest[5] can be a spiritually rejuvenating experience. Do you remember your first experience outside around a fire?

CLEARING YOUR HOUSE

It is a good idea to occasionally clear your house. This is especially important after a large gathering, a death in the family, a visit from an unwanted guest, a quarrel, or once a year during spring housecleaning.

Even a party—especially when it includes drinking or loud talking—can be over-stimulating because it leaves a variety of conflicting energies and thought-forms in a room when it is over. People with sensitive nervous systems or clairvoyant abilities often find they have trouble sleeping or being at peace after a fun party or a night of talking and mixing with different people. If your meeting was a religious or spiritual gathering that left your home with an uplifting or good energy, you don't need to clear it.

Motel or hotel rooms often keep people awake for reasons other than dripping faucets. Think of the hundreds or thousands of people who have slept in the same room! Sensitive people travel with incense and holy water to minimize these influences.

To clear a motel room, light a smudging herb, incense stick or, in an emergency, a cigar, and place it in a glass or metal container. Leave it to smoke while you open a window or door (this is important). If there is more than one room, you must open a window in every room. Incense sticks work nicely. If you travel frequently, take a spray bottle of holy water in your car and carry a sage stick and fireproof container for it. Use them each time you occupy a new room.

If a room is stale with cigarette smoke, then your use of tobacco won't clear the room and unfortunately may be a negative sign of former occupants that you probably won't clear with anything. Ask for another room.

This points out the paradox of tobacco. A little, like all powerful substances, goes a long way. Overused, it ruins or pollutes and may be a sign the room has a "history." Cigarette abuse and overuse has damaged property and people and ruined the image of tobacco in today's society.

To clear your entire home, smudge each room with sage smudging sticks or smolder incense in each room with a window open. The bad energy will go outside, where it dissipates. To clear a haunted, very old, or large house, smudging with sulfuric powder may be needed. Open all the windows and doors and vacate the premises to avoid breathing the smoke. Wear protective goggles and a painters mask or handkerchief over your nose and mouth.

Another method of clearing a house is to use a large iron skillet in which you scorch or burn salt and then walk around the house smoking every room. This method requires enough physical strength to hold the iron skillet aloft for a while using pads to protect your hands. Outside, pouring salt around the house's foundation is a Celtic method for keeping bad energy out as is their method of putting a mirror in a window in every room with the mirror side facing outside. If a ghost or bad energy persists ask a medium, priest, or clearing expert to help you out.

Other clearing helpers include lighting white or purple candles and using scented oils or incense such as frankincense and myrrh, playing chants or Christmas music through the house while clearing and requesting, through prayer, the removal of the undesirable energy.

Rooms change vibrations with the thoughts and actions of the occupants. Landlords need to smudge their rental property after the departure of a tenant, especially an undesirable one that had to be evicted!

 # PREPARING AN ALTAR FOR HELP

Spiritual or religious altars are frequently in the homes of successful people. To begin your communication with your higher power or, if you prefer, your higher self, prepare an altar. You will need:

1. An offering of sacred herbs, incense, or oil. For Indian spirit help, include sage, tobacco, lobelia, red willow, pinon, juniper, or sweet grass.
2. Your totem or a symbol of your totem.
3. A candle.
4. A bird feather.
5. A special rock, mineral stone, or gem.

6. A tiny portion of rainwater, mineral water, or holy water.
7. A favorite or beloved object.
8. A written prayer, request, or wish.

To be in the proper state of mind you need:

1. An emotional desire to improve your life and motives (for the good of all).
2. A willingness to "Let go, let God," surrender to changes in your life, to "Go with the flow," to quit trying to swim upstream.
3. The faith and knowledge and absolute positive *state of mind* that your path will be guided and knowledge about what you're supposed to do will be given. You are here on this planet for a reason—you have a *raison d'être*, or reason for being.

The objects for your altar, listed above, include representations for the four directions and for the four elements: earth, air, fire and water. The impetus, or force, that will make your prayer or request work are the three necessary emotional states. The necessary mental states help propel your energy along the desired path.

Negativity from you can undo even the most powerful ritual and request. In fact, some unanswered prayers are a result of a person's not being ready. What you believe will happen, happens, including negative outcomes. If you had a way of counting the fears and negative thoughts you give out on a daily basis (one estimate is sixty thousand a day!), you would understand the importance of always having faith in your dreams. Our primitive brain stem reacts only to preserve the status quo of primordial memory traces that are no longer appropriate for contemporary people.

To prepare your altar, place it in as private a place as possible. Leave it out or put it in a container that can be brought out easily. Use it daily, preferably morning and night. Native Americans and Eastern holy men often face their altars to the east because this is the direction from which the morning sun rises and begins each new day. Timing your prayers is

important, too. The new and full moons are seen as powerful times to start a new project (new moon) and to bring into fruition an old one (full moon).

Repeat your request or prayer aloud. Remember to add the words "For the good of all" after your request so you do not inadvertently attempt to manipulate another human being. Even when doing a healing for another, it is best to obtain the person's consent first or, if impossible, ask that the healing be done only if it is "right for the person at this time."

Sage, tobacco, or herbs such as sweet grass need not be lit to be an offering, but then another pleasant smell—a scented candle or oil—is needed. Burning tiny pinches of sage or small white sage smudging sticks are nice indoors.

For your home altar, use prepared incense sticks or cones. Pinon cones are a wonderful aromatic treat and attract Native American guides. Experiment until you find your favorite. Sandalwood is favored by angels and all spirit helpers.

Candles should be lit just before you use them and blown out as soon as you are through. Candles attract guides from the unseen world that surrounds us and are recognized by religions around the world for this purpose. Select from white, purple, indigo, blue, gold, or yellow candles. You need only one. Let your instinct or "knowing" select the candle color you use.

If you are requesting a healing for yourself or another, use or include an orange or a green candle. Red ones shouldn't be used unless you are in a depression that is not caused by a physical illness. For relationship or family problems, use as many as needed to represent each person.

Small candles cost more and don't last long but offer more color variety. Large candles in heavy glass bought at the grocery or religious store are the safest and least expensive. When home, keep a candle burning to remind you of your increased faith and strength and to attract angel helpers. Place your car keys by the candle so you will remember to blow it out when you leave. Do not place candles near blowing paper or curtains or where pets or small children can get at them!

Your altar may be covered with a special cloth before laying your implements on it, or it may be covered after each use, as you desire.

Wake-up Call: At your altar every morning, recite your desired wish, prayer, or positive affirmation.

Before Bedtime: Repeat your need for help or healing or your positive power statement right before bedtime. If you have time, light your candle or use incense in the morning and night.

◨ ROCK DIVINATION

The ideal rocks for divination should be between the size of an orange and a basketball. If they get too heavy, you cannot turn them over to use the other side (however, one side will suffice in some cases). Let your intuition guide you when selecting your stone. Ideally, you want to be in a location with numerous choices where you can walk around and select a stone at random. Before you pick up your rock, decide on the question that you want answered. Keep this issue firmly in your mind as you select your stone. When you see one that feels right, take it to your place of meditation or, if the rock is large, sit down beside it. Always return your rock to its original location when finished as it may be there for a reason.

In silence, meditate softly to your spirit guides and ask for guidance and vision. Relax your body and clear your mind of all thoughts. Use the method most effective for putting yourself in a meditative state. Remind yourself of the question to be divined. Take the rock and turn it around until one side appeals to you. Clear your mind now of all thought and focus on the pictures you see in the rock. Let your mind flow naturally. Without evaluating your pictures, state them one at a time as you see them. Beginners should write down their images or briefly draw them. Take your time and be creative in the process. After you have finished writing down all the pictures you have seen, turn the rock over to another side and begin again.

After you have derived at least ten pictures, state the original question you are divining to yourself and apply the question to each of the ten pictures. What could the picture indicate for the question? How does it apply? Is there a common connection between the images? Where is there a possible answer? Let your mind weave a solution from the pictures. All information may not apply in an obvious way, but delve deeply into hidden possibilities or solutions. Let your mind "free associate" (say aloud your thoughts to each picture without direction or censorship). Sometimes, the answer becomes obvious with several pictures. At other times, all of the pieces of the puzzle must be analyzed together before a solution appears. What was the answer to your question?

YOUR HOME AND HEALTH

Edgar Cayce, the famous psychic healer, recommended products for better health. The Heritage Store, in Virginia Beach, will send you a catalog that is full of wonderful, hard-to-find health items, true to the originals recommended by Cayce, and more.

Glass Cleaner: Use an empty commercial glass cleaner spray bottle filled with equal parts of white vinegar and water.

Cleanser: Bon Ami is the safest.

Detergent: Seventh Generation Brand, Broomfield, Colorado, uses only recycled paper. Order your paper products—toilet tissue, facial tissue, paper towels—in bulk from them, postage free, and quit having to shop so often. Recycled paper saves our trees.

Dishwasher Detergent: Lifetree automatic dishwasher liquid. You only use a teaspoon; it lasts a long time.

Burned Pans: Dump salt to cover burned places, then cover with white vinegar. Let sit twenty-four hours. Scrub out with brush. Repeat if necessary.

Insect Control: Order environmental garden supplies from Gardens Alive.

Lawn Control: Depending on your climate, think about having cactus or wild flowers as part of your lawn. Use plants for groundcover wherever possible. If you use compost on your lawn to build the health of your

grass, you won't need herbicides. Grow edible plants and herbs in your yard and garden.

Edible Plants and Useful Herbs: Lobelia, echinacea, yarrow, sage, pennyroyal, catnip, valerian, garlic, onion, mustard, sunflowers, juniper, nasturtiums, aloe vera, rose, ginseng, licorice, Saint Johns wort, parsley, lily of the valley, poke, lamb's-quarter, chives, and witch hazel are among the many herbs and plants you can grow easily and enjoy. *The Complete Book of Edible Landscaping*, by Rosalind Creasy and published by the Sierra Club, is appropriate for homes in a variety of different climates.

Garden Vegetables: Consider growing your own vegetables. Instead of putting vegetable and fruit garbage down the disposal, put it in a compost pile. If you aren't interested in growing but want to eat organically, order a catalog from Walnut Acres, a fifty-year-old organic farm in Pennsylvania.

Plants and Herbs in the Wild: If you are a hiker or outdoors person and want to eat wild plants, be sure you know what you're picking. Read up before you attempt trial-and-error identification, and avoid any plants with poisonous look-alikes. The book *Wild Edibles of Missouri*, published by the Missouri Department of Conservation, was written by Jan Phillips, who has tried recipes and gives you the results. In your own community, check bulletin boards for naturalistic groups offering courses in herb location and survival in the wild.

Green Supplements: If you don't eat green plants and herbs, help your health by taking liquid chlorophyll or a green supplement such as Kyo-Green everyday. Or try alfalfa greens, barley greens, spiralini, or other green products.

◧ HELP THE PLANET

Join a group interested in the welfare of your community or world. The Sierra Club attempts to watch harmful legislation affecting our forests (yes, it is still happening). It has chapters in every large city.

Greenpeace, Save the Children, and rain forest organizations generally

have 800 numbers, so there is no charge to call any of them for member-ship information.

Note: All brands, groups, addresses, and the quality of products are subject to change with new ownership, corporate mergers or changes of directors. Please assess all recommendations yourself and compare to sim-ilar products. New health supplements will appear as discoveries are made and, one hopes, present better-quality items. In keeping with the nature of this chapter, please make your own judgments, and keep the best of the old ways and add new methods.

Chapter Three

BODY

American colonists didn't know why the American Natives fasted, used sweat baths, purged, believed in cleansing the colon and, amazingly, believed in washing. The East Coast Indians who greeted the arriving colonists bathed daily, scrubbing with soft plants, while the colonists believed that sitting in water made you sick. Soap and germs were undiscovered.

Native Americans lived in a bountiful environment, had an established social system, bathed in clear streams or hot springs, were unified in their clan religion, and still believed they needed to undergo processes that purified the body from the inside out.

Early pioneers, escaping from religious persecution, starvation or criminal prosecution flocked, or were shipped, to the New World. They were hardly in a position to judge the "savage," a term used by early Europeans to describe Native Americans.

The savage medicine men, declared Father Pierre Biard in 1611, were "sorcerers, Jugglers, liars, and cheats. Moreover, all their science consists in a knowledge of a few simple laxatives—or astringents— hot or cold applications—lenitives or irritants for the liver or kidneys, leaving the rest to luck nothing more. But they are well versed in tricks and impositions."[6]

CLEANSING

In his book, *American Indian Medicine*, Virgil Vogel points out that there is no question that the American Indians independently discovered the enema tube and bulb syringe and that their use was widespread. Animal or fish bladders were used in conjunction with inserts made from small hollow bones or reeds. Vogel quotes early reports of Indian medical practice:

> Pierre Charlevoix was certain that the Indians were "in possession of secrets and remedies which are admirable".... "A broken bone was immediately set and was perfectly solid in eight days time." Of especial importance is his observation in 1721 of the use of enema syringes: "In the northern parts they made much use of glisters, a bladder was their instrument for this purpose. They have a remedy for the bloody-flux which seldom or never fails; this is a juice expressed from the extremities of cedar branches after they have been well boiled."[7]

Native Americans believed that purging the body was a necessary precursor to religious rites (for the shaman) and healing rites (for the patient), regardless of the suspected reason for the illness. Sweat lodges, fasting, syringes, and strong herbal mixtures promoted excretion of unwanted substances through perspiration (diaphoretic), vomiting (emetic), or ejection through the bowels (cathartic).

These cleansing practices, except for vomiting, continue to grow in popularity with certain health-oriented advocates. Enthusiasts attest to the benefits. If Native Americans used inner-body cleansing techniques, how much might overfed, underexercised, overmedicated, and chemically overloaded Americans need such methods! Yet they are generally avoided or considered unmentionable by the medical profession, including gastroenterologists, and the general public.

Dr. Bernard Jensen, an authority on colonics, recently gave a lecture

in the writer's hometown; at the time he was approaching the age of ninety! Mr. V. E. Irons, a pioneer colon-cleansing advocate and researcher, married a woman fifty years younger and fathered children in his eighties. Another enthusiast, Dr. Norman Walker, varyingly reported to be 106 to 116 years old, drowned while swimming in the ocean.

As noted in the chronicles of early settlers, the idea of cleansing the body inside and out was widely practiced and accepted by Native Americans. Soap didn't achieve widespread use in Europe until the mid-1800s, when Pasteur discovered germs. Colonists noted that Native Americans in the southwest and as far north as the Dakotas used natural substances such as yucca root (called soap root) to wash themselves, their hair, and their clothes.

Original sweating procedures primarily focused on healing a sick patient or preparing the medicine man or woman for ceremony or vision. Sweating was usually followed by jumping into a river, and sage leaves were then used to dry and purify the person. Fasting and colon cleansing routinely accompanied the sweat. Beverages with powerful ingredients promoted vomiting and visions, preparing medicine leaders for strenuous rites and journeys.

Navajo healing rituals often took seven days, during which time the sick child or adult didn't eat. It was believed fasting helped heal the problem; cooks in Navajo schools knew when a child was fasting and didn't serve the child food. Navajo medicine leaders today claim to cure people of cancer when traditional doctors have given up hope.

One of the last, older Dakota medicine men, Elmer Running, requires four-day fasts without food or water for his vision quests if the person is healthy. The true medicine healer will "know" the condition of the person he or she is treating and prescribe accordingly. Although Native Americans believe ritualistic healing procedures lose power if tradition is not followed, old methods, which blended over time with Christian elements, vary widely with each medicine man and woman, even within tribes. Remember, missionaries have been "saving" Indians for five hundred years, with the result that all have a mixture of belief systems. For this reason it is up to the person to choose a "shaman" carefully and not do anything that doesn't feel right. Pseudo-medicine men and women may have little information about safety procedures. Unfortunately, young Indian shamans don't always know the old ways because their religion, being shamed, wasn't learned. On the other hand, there are young Native Americans possessing divine talents and healing information received from above.

◨ SWEATING AS CLEANSING

Methods for encouraging perspiration varied with climate and terrain. Native Americans enjoyed bathing in hot springs if they were available. After a hot bath, one could bury oneself in mud for a healthy body skin mask or cool off in cold water.

Medicine men or groups of councils or societies used caves or sweat huts. River rocks heated in a center fireplace and doused with water send huge clouds of steam over the occupants. Rising temperatures brought on loss of body fluid through the skin. Sitting in a confined steam bath, whether in a lodge or hot spring, promoted sweating, a necessary procedure to help the body dispose of unwanted toxins.

Traditional sweat-dwelling openings faced the east as this is the direction of the rising sun. Today, the sweat lodge has expanded from the traditional use by Native Americans to being a popular therapy for anyone interested in serious cleansing of a physical or spiritual nature.

In certain states, such as Arizona, there is resentment toward white men who lead traditional sweat ceremonies, sometimes with good reason. Skilled native leaders have intuitive and spiritual communicative skills to receive help from nature beings, but these qualities may be absent in inexperienced or non-spiritual sweat lodge leaders. After hundreds of years of religious ridicule, Native Americans resent Caucasians "playing Indian."

The author saw an eagle drop a feather on one vision quest/sweat lodge led by an experienced, full-blooded Lakota, Gary Bear Heals. An

umbleche (vision quest) led by him brought on an unusual cloud formation that totally surrounded the camp. When you looked up, it was like a view from the bottom of a giant fishbowl.

On numerous occasions, the author has seen tiny lights flickering all around the ceremonial teepees of experienced leaders of Indian and non-Indian descent. With inexperienced leaders, there is more likelihood of the sweat being dangerous; for example, using the wrong river rocks could result in an explosion that injures the participants. Misuse of ceremonial procedures is considered sacrilege.

Generally speaking, with some exceptions, sweat lodges done by competent leaders of any racial heritage have contributed benefits to participants throughout the United States and Europe. The benefits of hot springs have long been known to Americans, as the number of visitors to these springs attests. In addition to the sweating process, hot mineral springs feed the body extra nutrients that are absorbed through the skin.

Participants need to monitor their own heartbeats as temperatures rise, whether in their own Jacuzzis or in formal sweat lodges led by an "expert." Some leaders think the hotter the better for spiritual growth!

The writer recommends wearing an illuminated watch with a second hand and monitoring your heartbeat during your first sweat. Tell your leader you want to sit by the door and may have to leave if your heart rate gets too high. This is especially important for people with heart trouble in the family.

As in aerobics, never exceed 80 percent of your maximum heart rate and always start with 60 percent of the maximum heart rate in a sweat. To compute your maximum heart rate, subtract your age from 220. Thus, if you are forty-eight years old, your maximum heart rate would be 172 beats per minute. If there is a question of safety at your maximum heart rate, don't go over 60 percent at the outset. For example, 103 beats per minute for a forty-eight-year-old (sixty percent of 172) is a conservative figure for the first sweat. For a person used to exercising and using good health habits, do not exceed 80 percent (138 for a forty-eight-year-old).

This heartbeat rate should not be allowed for more than twenty minutes in the first sweat, thirty minutes in the second. As your body gradually acclimates to the load of chemicals being purged and becomes less toxic, you will want to stay for the whole procedure.

The average person with typical health habits, or one who is over-stressed, will be shocked at how fast the heart rate accelerates if the sweat is a hot one. This is why a watch with an illuminated second hand is recommended; it is dark in a sweat lodge. For a quick reading, take a ten-second reading of your pulse by pressing the carotid artery in your neck or the artery in your wrist. Multiply the count by six to get a one minute rate. For example, heart rate of 17 beats in ten seconds is a 103 beats per minute, a 60 percent level for a forty-eight-year-old. If your heart rate exceeds your maximum, leave the sweat.

Fasting and colon cleansing will accelerate health gains, but for the novice should be done several days before or after the sweat, not at the same time. Perspiration sweats out bodily poisons that accrued late in our bodies due to the insecticides and toxins in our environment. Americans are on toxic overload. Prolonged sweats draw out toxins stored in the tissues, thereby reducing the risk of arrythmia brought on by their presence in the bloodstream. Starting slowly and working up to longer sweats is recommended. Begin by doing your sweat baths at home or in a friend's hot tub.

I have never heard of anyone having a heart attack or dying in a sweat lodge, so perhaps the guardian Indian spirits accompany those involved. The alcoholic and drug treatment movements have found sweat lodges and other Native American practices to have widespread effectiveness and healing power. Men's bonding groups are attending these sweats, as well as mixed male/female and female-only groups. Metaphysical stores and groups usually have notices or information for those wanting to try the experience. In addition to the cleansing aspects, the spiritual group experience is inspiring and brings unexpected rewards.

DOING A SWEAT CLEANSING AT HOME

If you want to do a sweat at home, to supplement your group sweat experience, you will achieve a positive health result. You will need the following diaphoretic herbs:

1. Elderberry leaves or berries to brew for a tea.
2. Peppermint leaves or cayenne pepper to flavor tea and increase perspiration.
3. Crystallized ginger, in candy form, to help you enjoy yourself and also increase perspiration.

Prepare your bed to protect your mattress from your own sweat. Take off customary bedding. Place a plastic sheet protector, shower curtain, or tablecloth across the mattress. Cover with a washable mattress cover. Have several washable heavy blankets ready on the bed to use as covers. Place several sheets or large towels by your bath to use when you get up.

Prepare your elderberry tea by pouring boiling water over the herb and letting it steep while you prepare your bath. Sit a potful next to your tub. Take as hot a bath as you can stand, or use your Jacuzzi. As your bath water cools, keep running more hot water into the tub. Drink as much of the tea as you can while you eat some ginger. Just as you do in any sweating procedure, time yourself or monitor your heartbeat.

When you get out, wrap up, take your teapot and ginger, go to your protected bed, and wrap up in your blankets. You will continue to sweat just as if you were in the tub. Stay there until you cool off, from thirty minutes to an hour. Stay quiet, sip more tea, and congratulate yourself on beginning your detoxification program. Afterward take a shower and use a skin brush or sponge to scrub. Don't plan any activities except quiet ones until bedtime.

◰ MUD BATH

Used in expensive salons and health farms, the mud bath can be done at home. If you live on a farm you can find a muddy spot and on a warm day cover yourself with the mud and lie out to dry. If you are an urban resident, you will need to purchase bentonite—natural clay. It is sold in bags in beauty-supply or health-food stores.

Choosing a warm day, or a warm patio, mix the betonite with water, and cover yourself with a thick layer on one side or one part of your body, unless you have enough to lie down in, in which case then cover up with it. Let the mud dry and then rinse it off outside. For small applications, buy the brand-name jars of bentonite and use it at night for a facial or for selected blemishes. Queen Helene and Aztec Secret Health and Beauty both sell jars of inexpensive clay packs. The psychic healer Edgar Cayce advocated castor-oil packs for certain parts of the body to aid arthritis and the organs. Just heat castor oil, pour on a soft towel, and apply to areas such as the gall bladder, liver, or colon. Using a heating pad over the towel will keep it warm.

◰ HEALING CRISIS

Trying any new healing or health method, when the mind firmly has decided on improvement, will eventually result in a process known as a "healing crisis." As unwanted chemicals and old deposits wash out, a person's body will go through an adjustment to change and have symptoms as the toxins leave the body. You may not notice it, and if you do, it won't last more than seventy-two hours, the natural time a body needs to adjust itself. For example, people on weight-loss diets notice that the scales don't reflect their loss for seventy-two hours (three days).

A healing crisis usually occurs this way: you will feel better immediately after doing a one-day or three-day juice fast. Then, after the body is "ready" because of newly acquired cellular health, clearing of the tissues begins and symptoms such as feeling a little out of sorts start to manifest. Perhaps you feel bloated or restless and think your efforts to improve your

health haven't worked. Sometimes you feel a little dizzy or get a headache, develop a cough, or have a discharge. Undesired toxins, chemicals, and other material have moved through the bloodstream, been secreted in perspiration, or been passed out through elimination from the intestines.

The healing crisis may go unnoticed if you are used to feeling out of sorts through poor health habits. This cycle of feeling good, having a healing crisis, and then feeling good again is a cycle that is repeated over and over until the body has cleansed itself. The body heals from the inside out, so after the colon begins to cleanse, organs in close proximity will do the same. You have only to remember that it is because you are strong enough that you can have a healing crisis in the first place because only a healthy body can continually cleanse and get healthier. You are adding years to your life span as you work on your health, provided you add the proper nutrients to your diet at the same time you do your cleansing program.

It wasn't because of "superstition" that Native American medicine leaders fasted and cleansed before ceremonies. *Cleansing actually changes the cellular structure of the body!* Spiritualists believe fasting and cleansing lighten the etheric and astral body of a person raising his or her vibratory level. This phenomenon explains why after fasting, people see "visions" or have glimpses of life in the unseen world. This is why Indians purged and cleansed.

Giving your child antihistamines to stop a runny nose or using antiperspirants under your arms every day actually stop the natural cleansing process of the body. For this reason, during your health-improvement program, please avoid taking pills to stop the flow of natural fluids in the body so the body can cleanse the lymph glands and mucous membranes. Wearing tight pants and bras that restrict circulation, and using talcum powder in the groin and underarm area are thought to contribute to the formation of cancer cells in the body. Babies can be powdered with cornstarch when necessary.

Use natural deodorants (available at the health food stores), not antiperspirants, and don't use anything when you don't have a reason. Save your antiperspirant for getting up in front of a group. Why would you feel a need when relaxed at home? Later you won't need them because your body odor will disappear.

COLON CLEANSING TODAY

Native Americans used devices to perform enemas to rid the body of trapped or undesirable contents of the intestines and for spiritual reasons (to make themselves purer in order to communicate with sacred guides).

Wealthy Americans used health spas such as those owned by the Kellogg cereal family, one of the first institutions to recommend colon cleansing and fiber consumption (the Kellogg brothers invented packaged cereal). Public figures such as Mae West and John Lennon were among those who valued colonics to keep them looking good and feeling healthy. Over the years and even today, movies stars routinely have used some form of colon cleansing to keep their figures and skin toned.

In 1979, *Cosmopolitan* magazine published the article "High Colonic Irrigation" by Carol Signorella, a New York City reporter:

"After a year of colonics, my appearance and energy levels were both radically improved. No more draggy mornings or late-afternoon slumps. The bags under my eyes had disappeared entirely, and the sallow, yellowish tone that had spoiled my skin has been replaced by a healthy glow. I seem to think more clearly now, and I need less sleep. In a word, both my body and mind feel marvelously clean."

The average allopathic modern doctor believes there is no toxic carryover from an impacted colon to other parts of the body. Medical tests that are available to measure blood contamination from the colon, as well as tests to find parasite contamination, are rarely used. One has only to walk through the drugstore and wonder at the shelves of laxatives to know that a problem exists. There are books that document the side effects of parasite infestation (common in congested intestines), but neither congestion nor its side effects are dealt with during physicals or medical visits.

One sign of progress has been the increasing knowledge of the value of increased fiber in the diet; health advocates have known about it for decades. When you begin to cleanse the intestines, you instantly feel better and the surrounding tissues get healthier. Fiber in the diet, exercise, and the desire to improve your health all begin to help cleanse the inner you. Unfortunately, spastic or damaged colons may not benefit from added fiber, as it builds up in the colon. Today various syringes and devices for colon cleansing are used: enema bags, professional colonic equipment in clinics, or coloma boards that you can use in your home. In the health-food stores, you will find books to help you learn how to use these devices. Recommended: Dr. Bernard Jensen's Book, *Tissue Cleansing Through Bowel Management*, and Dr. Norman Walker's book, *Colonic Therapy*. Dr. Jensen gives you specific directions for using a coloma board at home.

The importance of proper sanitary maintenance of this equipment, especially in clinics, can't be overstated. Once you are assured of this, health and chiropractic clinics have colonic therapists to help you. Less costly are home supplies that require some practice and education to use properly. It is usually worth the time and effort to learn the proper procedures to use at home so that you can maintain privacy and assure proper hygiene—unless you have more money than time. Good health-food stores carry the necessary supplies.

Herbal laxatives were used by Native Americans as both preventative and purgative measures. Herbal laxatives don't remove old, impacted colon contents but are useful for temporary constipation and purging. Colon cleansing attempts to remove impacted fecal matter and takes time and patience. It is not a quick fix, although you will think so after your first three-day fast (seeing what comes out).

Diabetics, cancer and degenerative-disease patients, or people with

abdominal pain or suspected appendicitis shouldn't undertake colon cleansing fasts unless they are under the strict supervision of an expert. Unfortunately, people with advanced diverticulitis (pockets in the colon) may not be able to tolerate the water cleansing internally, as their colons may be abscessed. However, early stages of diverticulitis can be cured, so this is a difficult call. Please consult your medical doctor if you have any of these problems. X-ray examination will show the extent of the colon pocketing if you want to make the decision yourself. As a general rule, the longer the existence of diverticulitis and the older the person, the more reason to avoid using enema procedures.

Dr. Bernard Jensen recommends drinking watered-down apple juice with fiber and supplements to help move out hardened material stored in the bowels. The one- or three-day juice cleanse is a modified type of fast. Directions about time sequences and any supplements needed should be followed. Fasting while taking psyllium fiber followed by pancreatin enzymes begins immediately to move material out of the cells of the body, including the intestines.

Start with the one-day or three-day apple juice cleansing program described below. A month later try a three-day juice cleansing. Six months later repeat the three-day procedure. This program is a modified version of Dr. Jensen's and is conservative. Once or twice a year repeat the three-day cleansing juice fast.

Repeat the colonics or herbal laxatives as needed. After the colon is strong and healthy enough to function on its own, you will know when it needs an extra cleansing.

A strict water fast is usually too hard on American bodies because toxins present in the fat and body tissues dump into the bloodstream during fasting. Water fasting also does not "pull out" undesirable contents of the colon because the necessary supplements to do so aren't present. The same holds true for ordinary juice fasting, which is hard on the body because there is too much sugar present and, like the water fast, the body has to "absorb" the toxic contents of the colon!

◧ ONE-DAY OR THREE-DAY CLEANSE/FAST

Materials needed:
1 large bottle of apple juice
1 container of psyllium hulls
1 bottle liquid chlorophyll
1 bottle hydrated bentonite
1 bottle apple cider vinegar
Vitamin C tablets
Calcium/magnesium supplement
1 six pack of 6-oz. cans of tomato juice or V8 juice
1 large bottle of pancreatic enzyme, quadruple strength. This enzyme is essential.

Directions for mixing your cleansing apple juice drink follow these suggestions.

For your first fast, plan to stay at home and rest or watch television. People think they will surely starve to death if they miss one meal, when in truth they may not be hungry all day and may have to force themselves to drink all five drinks. After one fast at home, you may work if you wish; if you are planning to do a three-day fast, work the first day, say on a Friday, and do the next two days over the weekend while at home or running errands.

Depending on your usual schedule, plan to drink the cleansing drink five times during the day. Add one six-ounce can of tomato juice in the early afternoon as juice or heated as a soup. Obese people should add another six-ounce can of tomato or mixed vegetable juice in the evening.

Schedule an enema or colonic at the end of each day and an extra one the next morning if you are continuing the juice fast. It is better not to have to prepare food for anyone else during the day, although some people do better not eating if they appease their food fantasies by cooking for others or rearranging their recipes (thinking of food, not eating it).

Cleansing Juice Recipe

Pour three or four ounces of apple juice into a large glass.
ADD:
1 tsp. chlorophyll
1 heaping tsp. psyllium hulls (stir well)
1 tablespoon hydrated bentonite
1 tablespoon apple cider vinegar
8 to 10 oz. of water to taste

Drink immediately, as fiber will thicken.

IMPORTANT: Drink another glass of water an hour after each juice drink, together with six tablets of pancreatic enzyme.

Take 500 mg vitamin C (once or twice a day)
Take 1,000 mg calcium-magnesium daily supplement

IMPORTANT: Between cleansing juice fasting days, drink the exact same drink, described above, once a day; omit taking the six tablets of pancreatin.

However, get in the habit of using digestive enzymes after each meal if you're over forty. For example, after a large meal try taking one or two pancreatic enzymes and another with HCL (hydrochloric acid) if meat has been eaten. For meals of fruit, cultured dairy products such as yogurt or cottage cheese, or juice, you don't need digestives.

REBUILDING COLON HEALTH

The body will rebuild itself only when it is strong enough to replace the cellular structure. It can heal and grow stronger only when it has the proper nutrients to do so. Eating complete foods that contain essential enzymes, vitamins, minerals, and amino acids feeds the glandular, metabolic, and endocrine systems in your body to keep you and your vital organs healthy. Herbal supplements contribute to healing. Cleansing per se does not do the repairing. It moves out pollution and impurities that block the rebuilding process. So to gain good health, you have to eat nutritious food. To help you in your cleansing and health-building program, eat from the following list foods that are kind to the colon, digestive system, and entire body. These foods are in addition to the supplements, herbs, and foods already mentioned in this book, and can be selected according to individual needs and preferences.

Cereals, soft and hot cooked, are excellent for the colon:
Oatmeal
Rice (choose parboiled for a complete food)
Corn cereal (polenta), cooked, whole-grain
Starchy, hot cereals (add wheat germ for nutrition)

Vegetables and fruits that are good for the colon:
Carrot, or other fresh vegetable juice
Carrots, and other yellow vegetables, cooked
Squashes
Beets (cooked fresh)
Potatoes, white and sweet
Avocados
Okra
Bananas
Papayas
Cantaloupes and other melons

Apples and applesauce
Mangoes
Peaches, apricots, and nectarines
Figs, dried

Breads for the colon (avoid white and yeast breads):
Sour-dough, rye, or cracked wheat flour
Corn tortillas
Sprouted grain bread
Unleavened bread products

Acidolphilus (supplements, powder, or foods rich in):
Yogurt (without sugar added)
Cottage cheese
Buttermilk
Goats' milk
Cream cheese (reduced fat)
Milk with added acidolphilus

Herbs to help the colon:
Senna (natural laxative)
Slippery elm (demulcent)
Aloe vera (demulcent)
Cascara sagrada (laxative)
Black cohosh (muscle relaxant)
Wild yam (muscle relaxant)

Herbs to help get rid of parasites:
Black walnut
Garlic
Sage
Herbal pumpkin or pumpkin seeds
Wormwood
Onion

An interesting phenomenon noted by people trying to improve their "spiritual vibrations" is that the body will "dump" unwanted contents as the person has the proper intent and begins following some of the procedures described in this book. Mind and body do work together to change cellular structure. From a physical standpoint, vermin prefer unhealthy, more easily invaded environments in much the same way that cockroaches like trashy living arrangements and fleas like weak dogs. Once a person begins to improve his or her health, stronger body tissue results and the pests find it harder to find a disease pocket in which to take up residence.

Anyone beginning a new health technique should begin slowly, use moderation, and continue until the desired results are achieved. Don't give up and abandon your good efforts; your persistence will pay off!

◧ Natural Plants and Products to Heal

1. Eat whole natural foods and you won't need healing.
2. Eat foods your ancestors ate that are also an appropriate fit to your body type and digestive system.
3. Use herbs for healing and you'll stay healthier.
4. Save modern medicines for emergency needs.
5. Cultivate an appreciation and reverence for all living things, including our Earth.
6. Whenever possible, eliminate the use of herbicides, insecticides, and strong chemicals in your home.
7. Patronize companies that specialize in herbal ingredients and that avoid animal testing.
8. Join an organization that benefits the children or vegetation of our planet (both young, growing things).

Healing With Foods and Herbs

Heart

To heal the physical heart, use hawthorn berry, capsicum, and wood betony herbs, and take lecithin, raw wheat germ, vitamin E, blackstrap molasses, cod liver oil, and brewer's yeast supplements. Garlic, and foods with potassium, such as bananas and oranges, along with kidney herbs, help to reduce blood pressure.

To heal the emotional heart, use flower essences and essential oils, such as rose, jasmine, and lilac. Use incense or take tinctures. Sniff flowers or essences in one nostril and exhale from the other. Reverse sides. Seek love by loving yourself first and then giving love.

Kidney

To help the kidney, use juniper berry, dandelion, parsley, uva ursa, corn silk, and yarrow, and eat asparagus, cranberries, and green vegetables. Take liquid chlorophyll and use apple cider vinegar and lemon juice in recipes and drinks. Fresh asparagus and melons rank the highest for beneficial effects. Watermelon meals, in place of any other food, especially at night, give the kidneys a rest.

Don't hold in feelings, as the kidneys store old fear and facilitate repression. Combat fear. Talking therapy helps release unconscious old memories and suppressions.

Adrenals

For herbs to aid the adrenal glands, see the Power Herbs listed on pages 111–122. Of them, licorice is the best healer; the others increase individual energy.

The adrenals, which sit above the kidney, control the "fight or flight" reaction that is a survival instinct. Regaining personal power over one's life greatly enhances the adrenals, as the need to fight for control is greatly diminished.

Liver/Gall Bladder

Take the herbs yellow dock, dandelion, parsley, barberry, and Oregon grape root. Use colon-cleansing herbs. Brewer's yeast (contains essential minerals), vitamin C, vitamins A and D in oil form, and lecithin supplements are also helpful. Tomatoes, or tomato juice, and mixed tomato/vegetable juices are excellent, probably the best food for liver cleansing as they stimulate bile production. Fresh red beets, radishes, and raspberries are also good.

Emotionally, the liver and gall bladder store up anger and keep old grudges. Emotional release of anger and consequent forgiving need to be accomplished for optimum health of these organs.

Brain and Nervous System

Nervines are listed in Chapter Five, Herbs, starting on page 103. To those mentioned, add chamomile, wild yam, lobelia, and passionflower to teas to help calm nerves. Gota kola, ginkgo, regular tea and coffee, and DMAE-H3, a supplement, increase mental acuity and memory. Calcium and alkaline food (sweet fruits, vegetables, legumes) and cod liver oil keep the acid balance in check, aiding nerves. Lecithin and vitamin E are essential for brain health. Whole cereal (with the germ), and sunflower and pumpkin seeds contain lecithin and vitamin E. Brewer's yeast, valuable for minerals, and the B vitamin complex complete the nerve foods.

For emotional health, be true to yourself and follow the road that allows you to do the things that are appropriate, rewarding, and relevant to you as a unique individual.

Lungs

Ginger, cinnamon, eucalyptus, capsicum, and lobelia mixed with mullein, Saint Johns wort, and raspberry are helpful herbs in food, tea, or capsule form. Okra, comfrey, marshmallow, and slippery elm help soothe mucous membranes. Cranberries, whole citrus fruits with pulp, lemon juice, onions, hot peppers, garlic, blackberries, and raspberries are foods that help clear the bronchial tubes.

Asthma and bronchial congestion are sometimes an unconscious plea for love and help. Take whatever means possible to unlock these love blocks in your life and to become aware of your own needs and what you do to prevent those needs from being filled.

Pancreas

More than any other organ, the status of the pancreas seems to be a highly individualistic matter, probably based on a combination of genetic constitution and one's eccentric personality. Pancreatic status appears also to be a result of hormonal and enzymatic functioning and interactions. Digestive enzymes containing pancreatin seem to be helpful to people over the age of forty. Juniper berries, licorice, wild yam, goldenseal, uva ursa, and astragalus may be useful. The latter is a naturally sweet herbal sugar. Dong quai, devil's club, and hamula-prodigiosa herbs may be helpful. In place of white sugar, using black-strap molasses, maple sugar, or honey will deliver valuable nutrients. Fresh sunchokes, or Jerusalem artichokes, are healing to the pancreas as no insulin is present until the tuber is older. Diabetics must consult their physicians before assuming new dietary practices.

The pancreas is a finely tuned organ easily upset by excesses. Heavy smoking and too much caffeine, cola, tea, coffee, or alcohol consumption are hard on the pancreas. Of all the cancers, pancreatic cancer is the quickest and most deadly.

Try to live a well-balanced life, exercising moderation. It is the writer's opinion that problems in the pancreas reflect a lack of flow between the vital chakras of the body—spiritual, emotional, and sexual. In Native American terms: a soul problem.

Sexual Organs

Dong quay is good for women, Siberian ginseng for men, damiana and kava kava for both sexes. Raspberries are cleansing, as are citrus fruits. The nervine herbs listed in Chapter Five, starting on page 103, are helpful. Although pumpkin seeds are especially beneficial to the sexual organs, wheat germ, oatmeal, whole-grain cornmeal, organic cereals, and any nut (peanuts, filbert, pecans, black walnuts, soy beans, sunflower seeds, sesame seeds) are recommended. Take vitamin E and wheat germ oil supplements daily for increased sexual efficiency. For sexual problems not helped with herbs and nutrition, look first for two problems: diabetes and heavy smoking of standard cigarettes, that contain saltpeter.

Once these possibilities are eliminated we must then mention the most frequent cause of sexual problems—relationship problems:

1. An unsatisfactory relationship where there is a lack of love or trust.
2. Not being in a relationship because of avoiding contact with the opposite sex or choosing partners incapable of intimacy.

In either case, look to yourself, determine what kind of a partner you need, and take the actions needed to change your life and yourself.

Stomach, Small Intestines, and Colon
Crucial to overall good health, as a lack of proper absorption from a healthy colon prevents good nutrients being absorbed and used by the body. We have dealt extensively with these organs in the earlier part of this chapter.

Best Supplements
For your health's sake, when you can't or don't want to take the time to eat the proper foods, use the following supplements every day if possible:
Kelp or dulse tablets
Wheat germ (dump on cold cereal)
Vitamin A, B complex
Vitamin B complex
Vitamin C with bioflavoids
Vitamin E
Lecithin
Multi-mineral tablet
Digestive enzymes after a meal

Drink the cleansing juice drink daily (described on page 70) adding one tablespoon of brewer's yeast to the drink.

Whenever possible eat vegetables and drink one V8 or tomato juice or have salsa daily.

Avoid white sugar, white yeast breads, soft drinks, candy, and snack foods such as chips.

Eat an apple and orange when possible.

Keep sunflower and pumpkin seeds (pipitas) with you to snack on, along with dried figs and prunes.

Experiment with eating foods suggested in this book.

Good luck, and remember—*you are what you eat and what you think!*

Chapter Four

FOOD

Native American shamans knew that various factors contributed to the effects of herbs or medicine on the body, and that healing is a complex process. We can't control our culture, heredity, and environment, but we do have control over our own health in terms of food selection. It does seem peculiar that large numbers of people have no concerns about how they treat their physical (or mental) bodies, even though they have to live in them for their lifetimes and suffer the consequences of neglect. Your health begins to improve automatically with a reverence for your physical self (desire to care for yourself) and the consequent actions taken.

Change in diet does not require expensive foods and can be accomplished by eating simply. The southwestern Native American diet of yesteryear, still the diet of traditional Mexican and Native American families, ranks supreme. It has the same balance of food nutrients recommended and recently "discovered" by modern dietitians. Corn, bean, and rice combinations contain complete proteins and the complex carbohydrates that are so important for good health. Corn is high in essential amino acids (needed for protein) except lysine and isoleucine. These are supplied by the amino acids in pinto beans, which in turn lack tryptophan and sulphur acids, which are supplied by corn.

Adding vegetables such as squashes, peppers, onions, tomatoes, avocados, potatoes, and greens makes a tasty and nutritious blend. Fruit and nuts round off the diet. Capsicum (hot red pepper) is an invaluable herb in the native diet that provides increased blood circulation and lymph gland cleansing. It contains high doses of vitamin A and is a cardiovascular healing agent for the heart.

Science Illuminates History

Corn might be the first crop cultivated in North America by Native Americans. Pollen analysis in soils reveals wild corn as early as 80,000 B.C.! The earliest evidence of corn planting dating from 3000 B.C. was found in New Mexico. The red kidney bean showed up in the same area several thousand years before the arrival of Europeans.[8]

By the arrival of de Soto in the mid-1500s, large quantities of maize (corn), beans, squashes, pumpkins, and sunflowers grew in the Mississippi Valley. Besides huge fields of crops, de Soto found large temples and palace mounds and "witnessed the arrival of male and female chiefs on litters carried on the shoulders of commoners."[9]

Wild foods added important minerals and supplemented farmed foodstuffs. Bone analysis of Prairie Indians showed that those who supplemented their diets with wild foods were healthier than those who ate only cultivated foods.[10]

Two of the valuable foods picked from the wild that stored well over the winter were wild potatoes (Glycine apios) and black-eyed peas. During their first winter in New England, the pilgrims are thought to have survived by eating wild potatoes given to them by the Indians.

After the Indians saved the lives of the pilgrims by showing them how to survive on the potato, in 1654 the settlers passed a typical law that forbade the Indians from digging these tubers on "English Land." For a first offense, a Native American was liable to be jailed, and for the second, whipping was the reward.[11]

The Indian potato (*Solanum tuberosum*), now known as the Irish potato, was native to the Americas. Word of the value of this plant spread quickly among the arriving settlers and, as early as 1635, it was taken to Europe and cultivated.

Interestingly, the Irish adopted the potato as their main crop in place of rye and wheat. This change eventually resulted in disaster when the potato crops failed and millions starved. When the English refused to help, thousands of Irish were shipped to America. Those who didn't die of starvation or disease on the ships joined Native Americans and Blacks as the downtrodden groups of the 1850s. Countless thousands of Americans have mixed Indian-Irish bloodlines from intermarriage when the poor, rural Irish moved into Native American territories. Ironically, the potato, which provided Native Americans a food supply for years, brought the Irish back to the people and land where it originated.

Anthropological researcher and herbalist John Heinerman reported that southwestern excavations by anthropologists Vaughn Bryant and Glenna Dean showed high concentrations of pollen from willow, desert sage, greasewood, false-mallow, parsley, Mormon tea (ephedra), and various grasses, including domesticated Indian corn. The importance of pollen (indicating flowers and fruits) in the diet of original Native Americans caused these researchers to label them "the flower people."[12]

Data collected during excavation of various sites inhabited by Native Americans in fertile areas such as the lower Illinois valley suggest they used the following herbs and plants for medicine or foodstuffs: tumbleweed, hops, pink weed, watercress, butterfly weed, American lotus, mayapple, prairie clover, dewberry, amaranth, cleavers, ragweed, milkweed, love grass, wild strawberry, spikenard, columbine, marsh elder, yellow oxalis, sedge, roose foot, Solomon's seal, cinquefoil, cocklebur, jimson (locoweed), lamb's- quarter, pokeweed, chickweed, violet, mustard, mint, and duck potato.[13]

Nuts grown in the area included acorn, hickory, hazel, and black walnut. Included among trees whose inside bark is edible are silver maple, green ash, and slippery elm. Fruits from the region included plums, grapes, hackberries, and wild persimmons. When they were available, Native Americans ate sunflower seeds (which are 55 percent protein), pumpkin seeds, pinon nuts, and any edible acorn or nut.

Melons of various shapes and colors delighted palates in the summer. Flowers from squash and melon plants were prized for flavoring stews. All the edible flowers, and the fruit parts of vegetables and plants, were eaten. In southern Texas, large concentrations of pollen from flowers and seeds were found in Indian ruins dating from 800 B.C. to A.D. 500. The pollen found was derived from yucca, agave, cactus, sotol, and mesquite.[14]

THE CORN CULTURE

As rice is to Asians and wheat now is to the majority of Americans, corn was to Native Americans. Today, the United States still produces more corn than all other countries combined. Iowa and Illinois are the two main states for corn production.

Corn, a true grain, such as barley, rice, and rye, is native to the Americas (wheat, barley, and rice originated in Europe or Asia). The corn kernels are the large seeds of the plant, the stalk like a giant blade of grass. When the Bermuda grass plant goes to seed, it is a miniature of the mature corn plant ready to harvest. There are varieties of corn in South America with cobs three or four feet high on a stalk the height of a tree.

Indians cultivated hybrid varieties of corn long before the arrival of colonists. When he arrived in the Americas, Columbus reported seeing cornfields eighteen miles long. He took dried seed corn back to Europe where it began to be cultivated.

Native Americans helped the early settlers to grow corn. Every schoolchild knows the Indians used fish or other organic products to help fertilize the soil before planting the corn. Different varieties of corn were cultivated, although regional preferences and climates influenced choices. The mature cornstalk produces tassels on top of the plant, and the pollen from these tassels unites with the corn silk to produce corn. By cross-pollinating the plants by hand, the Indians had created hybrids.

Flint corn was the variety planted in the Northeast, as it grew in the harsh New England climate. Flint corn dried hard and required stones to grind but lasted indefinitely, thereby assuring food stockpiles. Today it is used commercially as a feed for livestock.

Dent corn, grown by Indians in the southeastern United States, was so named because the middle of the kernel sank in when dried. In the Southwest, flour corn, which is softer, was preferred for the preparation of flat breads, such as tortillas. This flat corn bread was cooked until dried (like a corn chip today), or the corn was ground into flour to be preserved for future eating. An older variety of sweet corn, grown for centuries, might have been consumed by tribes at peak harvest, except in times of plenty when it was stored. Sweet-corn varieties bought at the grocery store today are still popular whether fresh, canned, or frozen.

All harvested corn was either cooked in the husks and then scraped and dried or dried on the stalk. Corn dried on the cob required longer soaking and cooking time but stored longer. The harder the corn variety, the safer it was from molds and wild creatures. Today's hybrid corn has a tough outer layer for easier shipping but is harder to digest. Eating corn tortillas or corn mush (polenta) is superior for obtaining nutrients and ease of digestion.

Corn was mixed with beans or other vegetables in stews or was made into bread. Adding wild greens, fruit, nuts, and meat, when available, provided an almost perfect diet. Today, vegetarians know corn combined with beans make a complete protein in a meatless meal. Corn, with about 12 percent protein, combined with beans, also about 25 percent protein, balance the chemical protein deficiencies in each.

Soaking cornmeal in lime water softened it for tortillas. Research indicates the lime provides the body with a powerful calcium supply for good teeth and bones. Indian and Mexican children on the native diet, considered to be living in poor socio-economic conditions, have teeth far superior to those of other children. The need for braces in upper-income families results from the lack of proper nutrients in the diet, one consequence of giving in to demands for advertised sugar cereals and junk food.

◧ SACRED CORN

For centuries, agricultural tribes celebrated to honor the corn crop, naming rituals after the being: Green Corn (planting), Maiden Corn (immature corn), Mother Corn (mature corn harvest). By far the most

important of the agricultural rituals was the Corn Dance. A Franciscan friar, writing in the seventeenth century, observed:

> If you look closely at the Indians, you will see that everything they say and do is connected with corn. They practically make a god of it. They indulge in so much conjuring and fussing about in their corn fields that they...behave as if the only aim in life was to produce a crop of corn.[15]

Even today, southwestern Pueblos, such as the Santa Domingo Indians in New Mexico, continue to celebrate ceremonially with the Corn Dance. In the spring, a four-day period of community dancing followed by a four-day period of fasting and prayer in homes are rites for favorable planting. The next Corn Dance, to thank the young corn crop known in some Pueblos as Maiden Corn, is in August. This costumed and important event is well-attended by surrounding Pueblos and open to tourists at certain times. The fall ceremony honors the harvest of the mature corn.

Corn was part of the coming-of-age rites and marriage preparation ceremonies for young women. Corn rituals, considered a symbol of fertility, assured the woman would have children, be able to cook and nourish her family, and be a good wife. The Pawnee mother routinely offered kernels of corn to the altar.

> Before they began their meal, White Woman made an offering of corn at the west. She took some kernels of corn in a spoon from Victory Call's bowl and offered them to the nose of the buffalo skull that rested on the altar there. Out of delicacy, she did not offer corn to the sacred ears in the bundle....[16]

Young girls weren't considered marriageable until they proved their skill at making corn tortillas. Young Navajo girls poured cornmeal into fireplace ashes to make a tortilla of perfect shape and flavor. To make flat bread, Hopi girls poured corn flour, soaked in lime water to soften its texture, onto hot, greased stones.

NATIVE DIET

Various well-meaning nutritionists, believing they know more about nutrition than their Indian or Mexican friends do, have tried to convert these people from their standard diet. The truth is that the natural Native American and Mexican diet, still eaten by hundreds of thousands of people, is highly nutritious. Corn, beans, onions, avocados, tomatoes, red and green peppers, cilantro (Mexican parsley), nuts, honey and dried fruit, combined with custards, eggs, and meat or chicken provide a more balanced diet than the average American's. Seafood or supplements to provide iodine and minerals are needed for those living inland.

The Cherokee, noted for their good looks, tall stature, and intelligence, originated along the southeastern coast of the United States, where seafood (and consequently minerals from the sea) was available. The same characteristics were true of the northeastern tribes, such as the Iroquois, whose national constitution was an important source for the writing of the American Declaration of Independence. Also nutritious were the diets of Natives in tropical climates, where fruit, endless varieties of plants, seafood and interesting game such as monkeys, lizards, and large grubs were available.

European settlers found the vegetables grown by the Indians to be colorful and tasty. Pumpkin was scraped, dried, and braided into "fast food" snacks to be easily carried and eaten on demand. Corn flour mixed with honey or maple sugar became a prized winter dessert. Dried fruit and berries lasted until spring. A combination of dried fruit and meat made *pemmican*, which was easily carried on long journeys or through the winter. Food dried by heat contains all the natural minerals and vitamins it has when fresh.

Squashes and pumpkins provided the mainstay of the vegetable crop. Roasted pumpkin seeds provided a treat known as *pepitas*; and dried corn, pumpkin, and winter squashes were hidden by agricultural tribes in case of raids by nomadic tribes wanting to supplement their meat diet during the winter.

There is evidence of arthritis and rheumatism in Indians, afflictions that are thought to have resulted from sleeping outside and performing hard labor in all kinds of weather (such as lugging a buffalo through the snow). Famine, drought, and living in harsh climates with dangerous conditions contributed to evidence of prehistoric disease. The Native Americans had no dentists, and evidence of tooth decay exists. However, dental problems increased in proportion to the quantities of the white man's diet consumed.

Fatality rates for Native Americans increased drastically during forced marches to reservations and imprisonment. After all the buffalo were killed by white men, the government fed Indians rations. They were forced to eat white flour instead of whole-grain corn flour or wild rice and sugar in place of fruit and honey. Today, Indians, just like average Americans, eat a diet not unlike the one they had to learn to eat on reservations, supplemented now by fast food and non-nutritious drinks.

Indians living on reservations have a 50 percent chance of dying of diabetes-related organ failure. Their diet bears little resemblance to that of their ancestors. Their physical constitutions are ill-suited to the white flour, white sugar, processed-food diet of modern America. Native American fry bread, made of white flour and prized today by everyone except health food advocates, was born from army rations and hunger.

◧ WILD FOODS AND HERBS

Unknown to the average "city slicker," hundreds of varieties of valuable herbal plants still grow wild in North America and in residential yards. The infamous dandelion and other weeds such as mullein, yarrow, poke-weed, and lamb's-quarter, are sprayed with herbicide. Herbs in demand, such as echinacea, which used to flower entire prairies, are threatened with extinction as company herb pickers try to supply demands for this free natural antibiotic.

Spring greens, known to the Indians and early rural settlers, were believed to clear the blood and revitalize the system after the paucity of

fresh foods available in the winter. Native American women gathered all the winter greens they could find and added them to the corn and bean stew. Greens such as pokeweed, wild lettuce, dandelion, lamb's-quarter, milkweed pods, wild onions, and any edible flower or green were gathered and cooked together. Supplies of wild onions, garlic, and other "weeds" were assured by cultivation by Native Americans.

Today, the greens and herbs mentioned above are known to be blood cleansers and to add valuable minerals to the diet. Other herbal blood and lymph gland cleansers are burdock, alfalfa, chickweed, yellow dock, sarsaparilla, chaparral, and red clover. They can be purchased in capsule or dried leaf form and are used to help combat disease. Greens eaten regularly as a preventative measure to stave off disease can be supplemented with stronger cleansing herbs to combat specific health problems.

It is easy, nutritious, and tasty to eat greens bought at your store. Greens such as beet greens, kale, mustard, collard greens, and spinach are available year round and not eaten enough for health's sake. Rinse the greens, toss them in a skillet (still wet), and cook a few minutes until tender. Southerners flavor their greens with ham or bacon and usually overcook them.

Farmers and rural Native Americans with their own land still eat greens, corn bread, and beans on a regular basis. They go out in their backyards to pick pokeweed greens for supper. If a friendly farmer offers you some pokeweed, please know that these greens have to be cooked—they cannot be served raw. Country people from pioneer stock often live to be ninety years old.

⬛ Nature's Way

Imagine the beauty and luxury of your own natural garden and a fruit orchard inhabited by bees making golden honey right outside your home. You wouldn't have to go far to find abundant streams full of fish and forests stocked with deer and game. Your buffet would be organic, full of natural minerals, and free of pollution and additives. What a paradise!

Only cold, dry, or harsh climatic conditions, or two-legged enemies, would deny the guarantee of daily abundance.

The Plains tribes had all the buffalo they could eat, but agricultural tribes sought their meat sources from the animals living in the woods and around lakes. Animals eaten included rabbit, squirrel, deer, raccoon, opossum, bear, woodchuck, porcupine, beaver, turtle, and wild hog. Birds sought for food were wild turkey, goose, duck, dove, and quail. All varieties of fish, including crawfish and the amphibian frog and turtle, were caught and roasted.

Natural foods are the best to cure or prevent disease by nourishing healthy cellular structures with nutrients such as minerals, vitamins, and enzymes. These, in turn, feed glands, endocrine systems, and nervous systems, which enrich blood and help vital organs.

Today, we don't want to go out to kill raccoon for food or have to scour for wild vegetables. It takes knowledge to obtain proper nutrients, but it can be done. American grocery stores are a marvel of plenty; the supply and variety of food available is unequaled in history. Unfortunately, temptation to eat nonnutritious foods is strong. The more altered the natural foodstuff, the less likely original nutrients are present. One result is that there is little cancer in agricultural societies compared to industrial ones.

Meat, a body tonic, is needed for strength and protein, especially for growing children and menstruating and lactating women, who need natural iron from red meat and high-protein diets. Sedentary adults do not need meat three times a day. It is a chief contributor to colon cancer and glandular weakness. Today, children and adults need deep-sea food for protein and mineral content. People who are particularly interested in longevity include sardines and salmon in their diets.

Mexican cheese is a healthy, low-fat cheese that is soft and easily melted. Until recently, it was available only in Mexican markets or southwestern grocery stores, but it is gaining popularity. Like tortillas, it supplies calcium.

Pepitas (pumpkin seeds) are a delicious snack for adults and children and a valuable anti-parasitic treatment. Increase their strength by combining herbal pumpkin capsules or raw pumpkin seeds with garlic, sage, and black walnut tincture. Pumpkin seeds are invaluable in maintaining the health of the prostate gland and female organs. Middle-aged men, along with the rest of the population, should use pepitas as a routine snack. Purchase raw pumpkin seeds at your health food store.

New flavored desserts, such as sopaipillas (white flour!), are a favorite dessert served with honey. Choose local raw honey for the best health benefits. If you were to eat a classic southwestern diet, you could then afford to eat a dessert of Indian fry bread or a sopaipilla.

Wild rice, a grain instead of a true rice, is native around lakes in northern states. It is a tall grass that grows in water and is harvested by hand from canoes even today and, thus, is expensive. The Menominee Indians in Wisconsin and Michigan regarded it as their main food source (it supplied 25 percent of their diet) and honored this plant instead of corn. It has the highest grain protein of all the cereals, furnishing close to 20 percent protein by weight. Fish and game supplied the remainder of the high-protein diet available to the Native Americans living in the Great Lakes region.

Today, gourmet cooks serve wild rice as an accompaniment to meat for visiting diplomats unfamiliar with the grain or serve it as a dressing with quail or duck. At home, mix it with regular rice or serve with vegetables. It is a versatile, tasty food and is also good mixed with cranberries or other fruit.

Jerusalem artichokes, also called sunchokes, a member of the sunflower family, had their name taken from the Italian word *girasole*, which means "turning to the sun." Mispronounced by other Europeans as Jerusalem, the name remains. The artichoke is native to the Americas and was taken to Europe by the French. Different tribes ate the root raw, baked, or boiled. The tuber looks like a cross between a potato and a gingerroot. The fresh root is prized by diabetics because it contains inulin (not insulin), that keeps its sugar from being absorbed by the body and has only about seven calories. During storage it builds up sugar that can be absorbed, reaching a maximum calorie count of about eighty per tuber. Today, Jerusalem artichokes are served stir-fried, boiled, or creamed like a potato. They are a good substitute for water chestnuts in recipes.

Unfortunately, many Americans' digestive systems are sensitive to highly nutritious foodstuffs, due to a diet lacking in proper fiber, essential nutrients, and exercise. These factors, combined with overeating, have caused people to avoid these nutritional foods because they cause "digestive disturbances." Slowly begin to build up your body and rebuild cellular structures. Cellular growth is a constant, ongoing process.

EATING NATURAL NATIVE FOODS TODAY

Corn

Indians used every part of the corn plant. Besides being the number one foodstuff, corn products provided diverse services. Warmed cornmeal with comfrey leaves provided a poultice for sores and swelling. Corn silk added to hot water made a tea or flavored stews. Corn silk boiled in water added flavor and nutrition. Native Americans used the ground meal to clean leather garments and cooked food in the leaves (like our tamales today). Corn oil provided relief for dry skin and scalp. Corn was made into hominy with wood ashes, into succotash by adding beans, and into pemmican by drying it with fruit.

The Spanish word for cooked cornmeal is *polenta*. It is eaten by people the world over, from tiny, low-income homes to five-star gourmet restaurants serving *haute cuisine*. It is easily prepared, inexpensive, and highly versatile when combined with condiments suitable for different cultures and taste-buds. Settlers observed Indians cooking it as a cereal and named it bear mush. Originally from the New World, it rapidly spread to Europe during the seventeenth century.

Cooking Cornmeal

For the purest and most nutritious polenta, choose organic, whole-grain, yellow cornmeal. Ordinary cornmeal found in grocery stores is degermed for a longer shelf life. Degermed cereals such as wheat or corn don't spoil and are not as likely to attract weevils, as they don't contain the highly nutritious "germ," or seed of the plant. Health food stores typically carry a number of whole-grain corn meal grinds and mixes, as do upscale food markets.

Polenta-Cornmeal Mush

Ingredients:
1 c. whole cornmeal
4 c. water

Stir cornmeal into cold water before heating on the stove. This is the secret to preventing lumps. Bring to a boil, stirring frequently. Follow the directions on the package for length of time. Unprocessed cornmeal will take about twenty to twenty-five minutes or until the raw taste is gone. Preprocessed grits or quick polenta cereals may cook in five minutes. The latter are handier but cost more and, due to processing, may provide fewer nutrients. The longer cooking and coarser grains require attention and time (for stirring). Polenta can be cooked beforehand and reheated.

When it cools, cooked corn mush has the interesting characteristic of hardening into any shape in which it was poured. It can be sliced when cold and, when reheated, will retain that form. Or it can be reheated and stirred back into a hot cereal. In Italy, it is cut into pieces and served with sauce, like a pasta. Gourmet restaurants use it for every type of dish, including desserts. Pour leftover cooked (and still hot) corn mush into a pan, glass dish, or cookie sheet that has the shape you want. Or leave it in the pan in which it was cooked and refrigerate until you want to reheat it.

Instant Breakfast Cornmeal Pancakes

After cooking polenta, and while it is hot, pour it onto a cookie sheet. Chill until the next morning. Using a can of the size you want the pancakes, cut the cold polenta into rounds as though you are using a cookie cutter. Heat the rounds in a little cooking oil and serve with applesauce, maple syrup, raw honey, or fruit.

To serve polenta as a main dish, slice pieces into pasta-like strips and serve them in place of spaghetti in Italian dishes, or use the round pieces like tortillas and serve them in a favorite Mexican dish.

Brunch or Lunch Polenta

Cook the cornmeal as described above for mush. Pour the hot meal on a plate, and add soft-cooked eggs and/or beans. Serve with green chili sauce, enchilada sauce, or tomato salsa. You can add sautéed chopped onions to any of the sauces. Leftover heated polenta can be used to save time.

Dinner Polenta

Sauté onions and garlic in olive oil and then add spaghetti or marinara sauce, with or without meat. Serve on a platter over cooked polenta. Garnish with grated Parmesan cheese. Or just serve polenta with a generous amount of unsalted butter and freshly grated Parmesan cheese.

Grits

Grits are a coarse cornmeal traditionally served as breakfast fare in the southern part of the United States. They are usually served with butter as a side dish. Gourmet yellow corn grits are available and contain vitamin A. White corn grits are the most common.

Corn-On-The-Cob

One of the best and most fun summer dishes is a huge platter of steaming-hot corn-on-the-cob. At peak season, try to buy corn at a vegetable

stand. Purchase as many ears fresh or frozen as your family wants to eat. Boil the ears in a large pot until tender; test at three minutes for young corn, four or five minutes for mature. Serve with butter, salt, and pepper. Use corn holders as handles if you have them. Chew kernels well.

Corn Bread
Experiment with whole-grain corn meal mixes or make your own.

Recipe:
Grease and flour an 8-inch square pan and preheat oven to 350 degrees.

In one bowl, mix together:
1 c. stone-ground yellow cornmeal
1 c. whole-wheat pastry flour
$^1/_4$ tsp. salt
2 tsp. baking soda

In another bowl, mix together:
2 eggs
3 tbsp. honey
$^1/_3$ c. corn or other vegetable oil
$1^1/_4$ c. buttermilk

Blend the dry and wet ingredients, using as few strokes as possible. Immediately place in a preheated oven to bake for 20 or 25 minutes, or until knife blade comes out clean. Butter and serve with beans and greens. Freeze leftover bread and reheat later in microwave on defrost setting, wrapping bread in a paper towel. For those not wanting to "nuke" their homemade nutritious bread, wrap in foil and heat in oven on "warm."

Indian Fry Bread
Make your Indian fry bread more nutritious by making it with all or part

whole-wheat pastry flour with a little wheat germ added.

Ingredients:

2 eggs

1 c. milk

2 c. whole-wheat pastry flour

1³/₄ cup white flour

¹/₄ c. wheat germ

¹/₂ tsp. salt

2 tsp. baking powder

Beat eggs, add milk. Stir in the rest of the ingredients and roll out pastry on plastic or floured board until thin. Cut into squares or triangles. Fry in deep fat until lightly browned. Poke a hole in the middle if you don't want the pieces to puff up. Or let them puff out and serve with honey as a type of sopaipilla. Serve fry bread flat or filled with pinto beans, lettuce, tomatoes and cheese, with salsa and green chili on the side.

Beans

The fastest way to cook dry pinto beans is in a pressure cooker. If you have several hours, cover the beans with water and bring to a boil in a pot. Boil for about ten minutes, remove from the heat, and let stand covered until the pot stops boiling. Bring the pot back to a boil, and then reduce the heat to simmer the beans until done, about two hours. Add water as needed. Cook with onion for extra flavor and season to taste after done. Southern and midwestern cooks season with ham, preferably on the bone.

Bean pots are handy for those who want to leave them on all day while they are away. Serve the beans with corn bread and greens for a balanced protein meal. Mash leftover beans with a potato masher and make them into a bean dip.

Bean Salad

Enjoy the two native bean varieties, kidney and black-eyed peas, in a cold salad.

Combine cooked and cooled or canned black-eyed peas, kidney beans, and green beans together with sweet green pepper or canned pimiento. Toss with a mixture of two tablespoons salad oil, two tablespoons apple cider vinegar, a little garlic powder, one teaspoon sugar, and slices from a large red onion.

Ten-Minute Homemade Enchiladas

In large skillet, layer enchilada sauce and purchased corn tortillas. Top with thin sliced onion and processed low-fat cheese or Mexican cheese. Heat until hot all the way through and cheese is melted. Use three tortillas, one small can enchilada sauce, two tablespoons onion and one ounce cheese for each serving. Serve with beans and guacamole salad.

Guacamole Salad

Chop up and blend together three avocados, one large tomato, one tablespoon lime or lemon juice, two tablespoon fresh cilantro leaves, and salt to taste. Add a tiny bit of finely diced jalapeno pepper, taste, and add more if desired for a hotter salad. Serve with corn chips.

Posole

Quick Method: Use canned hominy. In a skillet, brown ground beef, onions, red chili pepper, and a little garlic salt. Add hominy and heat.

Longer Method: Soak dried hominy overnight in water or use pressure cooker. If desired, use the bean-cooking method described above. Add same ingredients as for quick method. Tex-Mex recipes add a little tomato sauce.

The northern recipes are different in that they use pork chunks (cut cooked pork into one-inch cubes) added to the hominy with green chili sauce (it's hot) and cilantro or oregano.

Popcorn

Have a fun Sunday night supper at home with an all-you-can-eat popcorn night. Kids enjoy it and it will provide needed fiber they probably aren't getting. Popcorn can also be served in a bowl with milk for extra protein. For your adult friends, pop one-half cup dried popcorn in corn oil in which you have added one teaspoon of liquid capsicum pepper. Sprinkle with a mixture of regular chili powder (two teaspoons) and black pepper, or pour several tablespoons of melted butter over popcorn and sprinkle with several tablespoons of chopped cilantro and serve.

◰ The Pumpkin Squash Family

The pumpkin and its cousin, the squash, are valuable vegetables too often overlooked, except perhaps on holidays.

The prolific master squash is zucchini because of its versatility, size, and the number of squash produced by a single plant you could easily grow in your backyard. The word *squash* comes from an Indian word meaning eaten raw, as that was the way Native Americans ate the vegetable.

Soft summer squash was eaten off the vine or cooked with stew. Pumpkin was dried raw and braided and eaten when hunger struck.

Soft Squash

Cut summer squash (yellow crookneck, zucchini, yellow straight-neck, scalloped squash) into slices. Sauté in a little oil with a little water added and cover until tender.

For a heartier meal, mix sliced squash and a generous supply of sliced onions together in a skillet. Add canned tomatoes and cook until tender.

Winter Squash

The winter squashes are actually the product sold as canned pumpkin because of their superior flavor. They are best eaten as is, baked in the oven with a little butter, and served with maple sugar or honey. Just cut in half, lay the cut side down in a little water, and bake for about 45 minutes at 350 degrees. The spaghetti squash looks like a winter

squash but is low in calories and fun to eat. When you scoop out the pulp after it is cooked, it resembles spaghetti and is served with pasta sauce or butter.

Indian Summer Salad

Add to your food processor (shredding disc) about $^2/_3$ c. each of the following cleaned and peeled raw vegetables: sugar or miniature pumpkin, zucchini, parsnips, red cabbage, sunchokes (Jerusalem artichokes), and carrots. Add $^3/_4$ c. pinon nuts, walnuts or pecans if desired. Add about $^1/_2$ c. vinegar and oil dressing. Chill.

Baked Pumpkins

Pumpkins are great fun and good to eat if you buy the small miniature ones or the three-pound variety known as sugar pumpkins. The larger varieties make fun decorations for children and interesting serving dishes for meals but are not as flavorful when cooked.

Cut the lid off a sugar pumpkin, leaving about a 2-inch stem. Scoop out seeds, rinse out leaving a little water inside, and bake on a pie plate. For a three-pound sugar pumpkin, bake for about 1 hour at 325 degrees. If you are cooking miniatures, repeat preparation procedure but cook for only about twenty minutes, or until done. Children love these pumpkins filled with other vegetables, with pumpkin custard for dessert or seasoned with butter and honey.

Unbaked Pumpkin

For a great holiday or fun meal, cut the top off a "Jack-o-lantern" pumpkin, keeping the top and its stem to use as a lid. Let the kids decorate the pumpkin but don't put any holes in it. Remove the seeds and pulp and warm the pumpkin in an oven. Fill it with your favorite stew or thick soup. To make pumpkin soup, mix one can of prepared cooked pumpkin, one-half cup of whipping cream or evaporated milk, one small can of chicken consommé, and salt and pepper to taste. Serve the soup from the pumpkin.

Pumpkin Pie Cake

Grease and flour a 9 x 13-inch pan and preheat the oven to 350 degrees.

Spoon canned, prepared pumpkin pie filling (not canned pumpkin without flavoring) into the prepared pan. Sprinkle with one box yellow or white cake mix. Drizzle with $1/2$ c. melted margarine and sprinkle 1 c. of pecans on top. Do not stir. Bake 50 minutes or until tester comes out clean.

⊞ FRUIT, SEEDS, AND SEASONINGS

Watermelon

Experts' opinions about the origin of the watermelon vary. Reports from early explorers stated that they saw it growing, yet it is believed by others to be an import from Africa. Whatever the source, it is a valuable food and tonic for the kidneys and bladder, for reducing diets, and for doing modified fasts. Give your body a rest from food for a day by eating only watermelon. Because it contains fiber, is easily digested, and 90 percent water, it will help cleanse sluggish kidneys and digestive systems. Eat as much of the melon as you want any way you like during the day. Diabetics need medical advice for any type of fasting.

Watermelon seeds are an herbal remedy for the kidneys. Crush leftover dried seeds in a coffee grinder and brew in a tea. Or purchase your watermelon seeds from an herbal tea company.

Pepitas

Although raw pumpkin seeds are the best herbal remedy, pumpkin seeds that you scoop out of your sugar pumpkin are good roasted. Separate them from the pulp, and toss them with one tablespoon of light vegetable oil and $1/2$ tsp. salt for every cup of seeds. Spread the seeds out on a cookie sheet and bake in a 250-degree oven until they are dried out, about forty-five minutes.

For a nutritious supplement, buy raw seeds and eat them as a snack or grind them in your coffee grinder to add to cold or hot cereal. Add

ground seeds or wheat germ to children's cereal and they won't be the wiser but will be getting healthier.

Sunflower Seeds
If you live in a sunny climate, grow sunflowers in your yard for fun and then harvest the seeds to eat or leave them for the birds. If you choose the latter, buy yourself and your family sunflower seeds at the store to use as a nutritious snack.

Cayenne
(Capsicum frutescens)
Cayenne pepper is the hot red chili pepper used in Indian, Mexican, and Tex-Mex cooking. It is recognized as a valuable herbal remedy and food. It is a general stimulant and serves to aid digestion, increase circulation of the blood, help the heart's action, and keep lymph glands functional. It contains large amounts of vitamin A and minerals. Take it when you feel a cold coming on. Used externally, it stops bleeding. Used internally, a large dose of liquid cayenne might restore heartbeat after congestive heart failure. When eaten daily, it helps prevent sickness. Capsules can be purchased for those who don't like the hot taste.

Corn Silk
(Stigmata maydis)
Corn silk, from the corn plant, is one of the best herbal remedies for urinary tract irritations. It is a diuretic (helps expel urine from the body) and consequently lowers blood pressure. Women benefit from taking herbal capsules before menstrual periods to help reduce swelling. It is also useful as a demulcent (contains a soothing and slippery nature) and is helpful with constipation. As with other herbal remedies, it can be purchased in capsule, tincture, or natural form (corn silk from the plant).

Dose: Take several herbal capsules whenever a diuretic is desired or to help soothe an irritated bladder or bowel. It is a mild herb and can be drunk in quantity as a tea.

Cornstarch

One of the safest and most soothing, protective, absorbent baby powders, cornstarch is better for babies than talcum baby powder, which usually contains additives. It is also safer for men and women to use than dusting talcum powder in high-risk cancer areas such as the chest, underarms, and groin.

Chapter Five

HERBS

In the year 1535, Jacques Cartier, a French explorer, began to lose his crew to scurvy. When his ship remained frozen in the St. Lawrence River for four months, twenty-five men died of this disease, which began with bleeding sores. One sick crew member whose legs rotted limped across the frozen river to seek help from the Indians. He returned cured. Native Americans treated him with a recipe widely believed today to be brewed from a juniper or pine tree. The bark and leaves of the tree boiled into a mixture were applied as a poultice to the wounds and brewed as a tea. Cartier sought out the remedy and saved the rest of his men. That was the first known use of an herbal remedy given by the Indians. We know today scurvy is a result of a vitamin C deficiency (ascorbic acid) in the body.

They came and gave an herb to me and said: 'With this on earth you shall undertake anything and do it.' It was the day-break-star herb, the herb of understanding, and they told me to drop it on the earth. I saw it falling far, and when it struck the earth it rooted and grew and flowered, four blossoms on one stem, a blue, a white, a scarlet, and a yellow; and the rays from these streamed upward to the heavens....[17]

NATURAL COMPOUNDS

Certain recently discovered herbal products considered "new," such as pycnogenol—a substance made from a French maritime pine bark—perhaps contain ingredients similar to the Great Lakes pines or junipers that cured the French explorers of scurvy. The French sailors had to learn from foreign natives about ingredients from trees like their own that would have prevented the scourge common at sea.

A similar situation exists today. We have the knowledge to prevent many diseases, but people and institutions tend to ignore the obvious and companies like to endorse products that sell. We can use the preventive approach to well-being by eating healthy foods that contain essential nutrients and by using herbs and supplements readily available to all. American bodies are basically starved of essential minerals and need vitamin and nutritional supplements.

Dr. Linus Pauling, a Nobel Prize winner who died in 1994 at the age of 93, for years advocated massive doses of vitamin C as a preventative health measure. The value of vitamin C was commonly ignored at the time; and was rarely recommended in a doctor's office, as Dr. Pauling was considered to be eccentric in his beliefs. Vitamin C can be purchased almost everywhere, is inexpensive, and can be taken in large doses without any ill effects. Dr. Pauling advocated 10,000 mg a day, took it himself, and outlived all his colleagues.

However, if we go cutting down ancient trees in rain forests and wilderness areas to cure people with their natural chemical substances, such as pycnogenol, we will creates future problems. These areas protect and provide food and environment for the wildlife in the region, are esthetically important as nature's gifts, and are crucial to our health. The trees preserve the ozone layer so we can go out in the sun without getting dangerous radiation. Wooded areas emit gasses that are critical to the ecological balance of Earth's atmosphere. Vegetation preserves stable climatic conditions, preventing a dangerous melting of the ice caps, which could tilt our planet's axis.

Commonly known health habits such as eating fruits and vegetables and using natural remedies from plants reduce health problems. If we eat better diets and improve our thoughts and actions to help ourselves and others, the body won't need unusual products to help prevent collapse of an organ or the immune system. The great forests can then be tapped conservatively for the supply of exotic herbal plants for those in need.

Plant products such as grapefruit seed extract are readily available. Grapefruit seeds contain ingredients known to protect against cancer-causing free radicals in the body. Grapefruit seed extract also has been "discovered" to be a natural preservative for cosmetics and foods and to cause few of the detrimental side effects caused by the nitrates and sulfates common in packaged fresh food and produce. Using this easily extracted ingredient from grapefruit will encourage planting trees instead of cutting down forests and, at the same time, provide a natural, safe preservative.

Modern analysis of the chemical composition of plants documents their proper use by the Indians. Synthetic duplication of compounds found in them accounts for numerous over-the-counter and prescription medicines. Diazepam, known by the trade name Valium, was synthesized from components of the native herb valerian and became one of the overprescribed drugs of the twentieth century. Valium overdoses accounted for thousands of emergency room visits, addictions, and deaths during the decades it was in vogue with doctors.

It is easier to write a prescription for "nerves" than to take the time to ask about problems in the person's life. Sometimes the patients are at fault, since they will use every means possible to get doctors to prescribe pills rather than make changes in themselves or their environment.

Natural compounds can be chemically duplicated in the laboratory. Although synthetic products are stronger and more effective in emergencies, they are easily misused. Pharmaceutical drugs lack certain enzymes and elements needed for optimum health. Today, people treat physical symptoms in isolation, disregarding the nutritional needs of the

body. For example, a headache is killed with painkillers; no attempt is made to discover and cure the underlying cause of the headache, which is only a symptom of a problem in the mind or body. Curing and treating symptoms is known as *allopathic medicine* and is the type practiced by our established medical system.

⊟ ALLOPATHIC OR NATUROPATHIC?

Contemporary allopathic medicine has saved many lives and is necessary in our hectic and increasingly unhealthy environment. For example, miracle surgeries after accidents and to preserve and lengthen life spans through organ transplants are wonders of contemporary medicine that provide hope and healing. Antibiotics, used wisely, are lifesavers and one of the modern miracles of scientific drug discovery. When the body's immune system has deteriorated to a certain critical point, drug compounds and unusual procedures are necessary to sustain life.

Overuse of prescription drugs, however, is one of the chief causes of illness and death in the elderly. The drugs, often working against each other, clog or undermine the body, making it harder for the natural healing process to take place.

> No physician worth his or her salt should insist on synthetic drugs for a patient, if the person being treated prefers herbs and natural medications instead. Synthetic drugs kill more people than herbs do. Unfortunately, we never hear about such matters unless they appear in some kind of statistical form—'An Estimated 27,900 Americans Die Every Year from Prescription Drugs!'—as a column 'filler.' ...But let one or two persons die from the misuse of herbs and immediately the rare tragedy is screamed all over the front page in bold headlines....[18]

Allopathic doctors attempt to cure cancer caused by toxic overload by giving the body even more chemicals. Chemotherapy and radiation

using poisonous substances kill healthy tissue as well as cancers.

Despite billions of dollars spent in research, little progress has been accomplished in curing cancer, with the exception of a few select types of cancers treated with substances extracted from plants! For example, *Vinca rosa*, a relative of the periwinkle plant, contains alkaloids, which are used to create one of the few documented powerful drugs found to arrest or "cure" certain leukemias and lymphomas. The composition of the alkaloids arrests cancer cell multiplication by binding them to a protein found in the cells. This progress in the cure or remission of these cancers appears to be about the only actual headway in curing cancer after millions and millions of dollars spent and time wasted.

Progress has also been made with sophisticated machines and tests that show early development of cancerous or diseased tissue. Although early detection isn't a cure, it raises a patient's chances of successful treatment.

In past years, good health knowledge was limited, at best. Today there is more health information available than a person can read. It is necessary to focus on your own health situation and take action yourself. If you have cancer or a serious disease, it is best to study your own health situation. Buy a physician's *Merck Manual* (published by Merck Sharp & Dohme Research Laboratories), talk to naturopathic doctors, read natural healing books, converse with your conventional medical doctor, and decide for yourself what you want to do.

Follow the above advice so you can have the best of both worlds (allopathic and naturopathic) in attacking your disease. If you are taking prescription medicine for any health problem, buy yourself a *Physician's Desk Reference*, known as the PDR, published by Medical Economics, and talk to your doctor about the drugs you are taking.

To prevent the occurrence of illnesses, start a natural health program as suggested in this book. Continue to keep current by reading and learning all you can.

USING NATURE'S HERBS

Herbs, like all organic matter, offer specific vitamins, enzymes, minerals and other beneficial effects yet to be discovered. Each plant used in healing has its own unique chemical atomic composition: a combination of molecules consisting of a particular arrangement of electrons revolving about a nucleus containing protons and neutrons.

Specific herbs and plants have vibrational levels attributed to their unique organic compounds and are drawn magnetically to similar elements. Certain herbs have an affinity or attraction to certain parts of the body and tissues and contribute nutrients and healing properties to that area or organ. This is one of the principles, besides nutrients and resultant effects, that determine what herb is good or beneficial for which part of the body. For example, nervines such as valerian are so named because they heal the nerves. Dandelion is a natural cleanser for the liver.

Deep-sea fish vary in their mineral content. Shrimp naturally attract traces of arsenic, a mineral found in the ocean and in small quantities in the body. Overeating shrimp can make you feel queasy from ingesting too much arsenic at once. In addition, natural shrimp breeding grounds are ocean shelf-beds, which may be contaminated by industrial waste dumping grounds.

Commercially cultivated shrimp farms are numerous today. Thousands of harvestable shrimp are jammed into overcrowded spaces with their own excrement and rotting leftover feed. To combat disease, they are overdosed with pesticides and antibiotics. Several years later, the land used is poisoned and barren. For your best bet for safe shrimp, ask for "turtle-safe" shrimp at your market. This will help ensure that endangered sea turtles have been released from nets and that the shrimp have been caught at sea (hopefully in the purest water). One hopes all shellfish (they are scavengers) will have healthy environments in the future.

Americans as a whole aren't easily treated with herbal compounds. Their bodies are on chemical overload from pesticides, insecticides, food preservatives, toxic cleaning agents, and work-related environmental

contaminants. Add to that individual weaknesses in the body brought on by a high-stress environment, and increasingly weak genetic constitutions from generations of eating over-processed foods. The poor nutrients and minerals provided by such foods starve glands and organs. The result is a diminished effectiveness of any healing agent, including herbal remedies. For example, pressure from an impacted colon and a lack of natural hormone production reduce the effectiveness on the uterus of the herb black cohosh, which is a natural relaxant for cramping of the female organs.

The strength of any herb will depend on nutrients present in the soil, the effectiveness of preservation techniques, whether the herb was sprayed or radiated and even, perhaps, whether it was picked at the right time. The effects of an herb's healing properties can vary widely between patients, and are influenced by the individual's physical and mental health.

If there were one single deficit in American diets that contributes to countless disease states, it would be a lack of minerals. Minerals are found in vegetables and plants and are highly concentrated in the sea, where mineral content has been leached from the land and concentrated in the water. These minerals are assimilated into fish and sea plants such as seaweed. People with sufficient income and without next-door, fast-food restaurants such as may be found in areas of Japan, do not suffer from mineral deficiencies. In the United States, Hawaiians have the longest life span, possibly due to the minerals in the seafood eaten and in the soil of the island.

Laboratory-designed processed foods often lack the natural minerals needed to feed vital glands and organs. Processing not only cheats you of natural enzymes but also adds toxins and stresses the body. These factors result in a suppressed immune system that lacks the nutritional support to fight disease. Vital endocrine, glandular, and blood-cell deficiencies ensue. Poor immune systems have set the stage for new immune disorders such as AIDS.

Native Americans healed faster than Europeans using herbal remedies because they were better nourished and believed in the spiritual sacredness of their environment and their bodies. Native Americans believed animals and plants were nourishing and curing gifts from their god. Healing yourself requires more than taking an herb or treating a physical symptom. Today, countless Americans don't seem to care what they do to their bodies. Diets contain too few minerals and too much fat and sugar. There is little interest in purging and cleansing the body for either spiritual or physical reasons. Optimum health requires a certain thinking or mind-set, a belief in the sacredness of your own body: *The body is the temple of your soul.*

POWER HERBS

Experiment with power herbs to see if they can be useful. Begin with one or two at a time, and use them long enough to determine their effects before you try another. Read the descriptions and choose one that seems to "call out" to you. Muscle-test the effectiveness of the herb if you wish. Remember, herbs are drugs if they have an effect on the body. Use them in moderation. As with all herbs and foods in general, diabetics should always check with a medical doctor before use.

MUSCLE TESTING

If you have a friend or health practitioner who does muscle testing (kinesiology), have him or her test the herb on you before using to verify its effectiveness on your body. If you don't have the herb with you, write down the name of the herb or product on a piece of paper and test with that while holding the paper in your right hand. Have a friend supply gentle energy to your left arm as it is extended parallel out from your body to the side at about shoulder height, with your elbow straight and your palm down. Let your friend gently apply pressure slightly above your left wrist to test your natural strength. Push up and down so it is obvious how much natural pressure your arm takes.

Test several herbs or products at the same time, and choose at random so you won't know which is being tested. Close your eyes or fold the

paper over so you can't read the names. If your arm holds strong, the herb would be good for you or helpful. If your arm weakens, the herb will weaken or not be effective.

For a large person testing a small one, subtle pressure is applied as, obviously, a brawny person could force down a weaker person's arm if he or she wanted to induce a false negative. To test the muscle-testing process before the herb test, write "table sugar" on a piece of paper (arm will weaken) and a power food like "raw wheat germ" or "sardines" on another (arm should hold firm, except in a case of allergy) so you can have proof that the test works. Muscle testing can be used on any food or medicine.

Ginseng
(Panax quinquefolium)
Shaped like male genitalia, ginseng was regarded by some as an aphrodisiac and accounted for many a tale of longevity and potency. The power of this herb, if for no reason other than the positive thought energies that surrounded it over the centuries, is considerable. The Chinese called the root *Jin-chen*, which means "like a man." The American Indian name for the plant was *garantoquen*, which means "the big man".

Although ginseng never achieved popularity with Native Americans as a wonder herb, as it did with the Chinese, both groups used the Panax genus for treating similar ailments on continents thousands of miles apart. Both the Chinese and East Coast Indian tribes like the Delaware used it to treat "female" problems, to increase fertility in men, to treat sores in the mouth and throat, to help coughs, and as a general tonic to maintain or restore good health. Medicine healers used it for love potions and to increase the power of other healing herbs. Because of foreign demand for the herb, Native Americans traded it with Europeans.

Today, the wild herb is threatened with extinction on three continents, especially Asia. It is grown commercially, but its slow growth makes it pricey. It is currently added to health drinks and sold in bottles resembling soda pop. It is also sold as an energizer in tablet and capsule

form. Experiment and draw your own conclusions.

Hawthorn Berry
(Crataegnus oxyacantha)

This herb is included because it nurtures a strong heart—the power center of the body. Native Americans used hawthorn berry to treat a variety of ailments, including female problems and wounds, as well as for a heart tonic. It was also eaten as a food. Today it is thought to dilate the coronary blood vessels enough to help build up the wall of the heart muscle. It also tones muscle tissue in other areas of the body, and athletes include it in their vitamin regimen. The herb is readily available in health and grocery stores. Try it for emotional wounding of the heart and grieving. Use in capsule or tincture form. The regular dosage is two capsules twice a day, or one dropperful of hawthorn tincture once or twice a day.

Licorice
(Glycyrrhiza glabra)

Licorice root, used by Native Americans to flavor teas, tobacco, and other foods, assisted in healing coughs and physical problems in general. Because it has a sweet taste, it was a favorite addition to drinks.

Today we know it contains a natural cortisone and consequently aids the body in healing in general. The cortisone in our bodies is regulated by the adrenal glands. Herbalists believe licorice helps the adrenals and the pancreas to regulate blood sugar levels and stress reactions. Americans tend to live high-stress lives and exhaust their adrenal glands prematurely. People who use synthetic cortisone or steroids, prized by weight lifters and other people interested in increasing their physical power and musculature, experience serious side effects with long-term use. Steroids eventually begin to have the opposite effect, tearing the body down as damage is done to tissue and membranes.

Licorice can be purchased in herbal or candy form. Don't believe licorice candy actually contains licorice unless you check the label, as

ordinarily the candy is artificially flavored. Don't buy it heavily sweet-ened because large amounts of sugar will negate any benefits to your pan-creas. Use the candy as a treat and, if in need of healing, take capsules or brew licorice leaves into a tea. No herb with natural cortisone should be taken in doses large enough to produce headaches after use.

Saw Palmetto
(Serenoa serrulata)
Indigenous to southern portions of the United States, saw palmetto is now available in health food and grocery stores in capsule and leaf form. Native Americans discovered that animals that ate the berries appeared healthier. Consequently, they ate saw palmetto berries and used them to treat a vari-ety of disorders ranging from digestive problems to mental tension.

Saw palmetto has a propensity to soothe and heal mucous membranes and may regulate and cleanse the female and male sexual organs. Herbalists recommend it for middle-aged and older men to prevent prostate problems. Some women find that it increases their breast size and may add curves. It appears to have a magical "balancing effect" on the male and female parts of the anatomy. In other words, it makes the body more attractive by adding curves to thin bodies and redistributing fat in heavier bodies.

Saw palmetto may increase sexual performance and frequency. The essential oil in the berries may regulate hormonal functioning or just keep sexual organs cleansed enough to keep them healthy. Because the lower part of the body is where the grounding, or foundation, of your body is located, this herb can only help your power base. Follow dosage directions on the bottle and adjust according to your own experience. Depending on your age and physical condition, results will vary.

Wild Yam Root
(Dioscorea villosa)
Wild yam eased colic in Indian babies and sore joints in their elders. Today we know that wild yam, especially the Mexican variety, contains

natural cortisone. Like licorice, wild yam root is a natural healer and is recommended for all types of physical problems. In herbal formula remedies, it is sometimes combined with raw adrenal gland extract.

Yam root has the added advantage of being a relaxant and has antispasmodic properties that make it soothing. Like all powerful herbs, dosage should be regulated and more doesn't mean better. Unfortunately, its popularity and well-known healing properties have increased demand for this herb so it is now expensive—unless you compare it to prescription-drug costs. The suggested dosage for an average person is one or two capsules a day. People with health problems should take twice that amount. The tincture is the easiest to take and absorb. Take one half a dropper once or twice a day. Like all powerful herbs, it should be kept out of the reach of children.

NATIVE AMERICAN WONDER HERBS

Barberry
(*Berberis vulgaris*)
and
Oregon Grape Root
(*Berberis aquifolium*)

More than one hundred species of shrubs make up the family of Berberidaceae, of which these two species are members. They are similar in composition and characteristics. Both are excellent antiseptics, blood thinners, and tonics for the body. Like the above-mentioned herbs in this category, the Indians used them externally for numerous healings of wounds and abrasions and for treating chronic diseases internally. They cleanse the liver and gall bladder by increasing the production of bile and the kidneys by cleansing the blood. The production of bile has a laxative effect and a stimulating effect on the thyroid gland.[19] Oregon grape root

is sometimes combined with antispasmodics such as wild yam, valerian and black cohosh to cleanse while relaxing the organs.

Black Cohosh
(Cimicifuga racemosa)

Black cohosh, known to Native Americans as snakeroot, was used by them for snakebite. Interestingly, it is known today to reduce high blood pressure, an effect that, one would assume, would reduce the speed at which snake poison circulates in the body. In addition to its value as a treatment for snakebite, Native Americans gave it to women in child-birth and those with menstrual difficulties, as it helps subdue spasms. It often went by the name squawroot.

Black cohosh is included in this section, instead of in the herbal nervine list at the end of this chapter, as it is more than just an antispas-modic: It is an "all-around" wonder herb. Rather strong, it will produce nausea or headaches if used in high doses. Because individual tolerances vary, start with one capsule or one-half dropper of tincture and increase as tolerated to two or three times that amount daily or as needed.

Today black cohosh is used to treat high blood pressure, asthma, res-piratory infections such as bronchitis, spastic conditions in the colon and duodenum, and nervous conditions. Take it in combination with mullein to treat asthma and with other antispasmodic nervines such as lobelia, valerian, or skullcap, as a relaxant. Reduce the quantity when you com-bine it with other nervines.

Burdock
(Arctium lappa)

The original burdock variety (Arctium minus), used by the Cherokee Indians for swollen and ulcerated leg wounds,[20] was replaced in herbal arsenals by the lappa species from Europe. According to Melvin Gilmore, it grows wild along old traffic routes used by early military and civilian travelers:

It has been adopted by the Indians for medicinal use. White Horse, of the Omaha, gave information…obtained from the Oto, of a decoction of the root being used as a remedy for pleurisy.[21]

The Russians also recognize it as a diaphoretic and use it to treat water retention, to provoke sweating, to remove toxins, and to cleanse tissue.

Burdock is also recognized as a valuable blood and lymph gland cleanser. Another cleanser for mucous membranes, this valuable herb is also a demulcent, which means it soothes tender skin and membranes by relieving inflammation. Skin eruptions, fever blisters, genital or intestinal irritations, and any other mucous membrane problem may be helped. John Heinerman, in *Science of Herbal Medicine*, states that burdock breaks up waste material in the bloodstream so it can be eliminated through the kidneys and is therefore helpful for arthritis.

Any part of the plant can be used safely. In countries that need it, it is used as a food. For the rest of us, capsules bought at health food stores can be swallowed or broken apart and used externally on the skin. For naturalists, your dog may help you find it in the wild by picking up burrs on its coat. Combine burdock with an equal amount of goldenseal for a stronger antiseptic but less soothing mixture.

Chaparral
(Larrea divaricata)

Chaparral, a creosote bush, belongs to a large varied group of southwestern plants. It is an antiseptic herb that has been used for everything and is not associated with a cure for any particular disorder except one. As reported by Alma Hutchens:

> Indians of the south-western areas used the plant as varied symptoms prevailed…in October 1967, after three previous surgically removed growths, an eighty-five-year-old man refused medical

treatment on the… fourth-recurrent growth, documented as malignant melanoma, in favour of 'Chaparral tea', an old Indian remedy. Of this tea he drank 2–3 cups a day. In September 1968 he was re-examined at the Medical Centre, Utah, U.S.A., which found that the growth had decreased from the size of a large lemon to that of a dime. No other medication was used…. In eleven months he gained a needed 25 lb., with improvements in general health…[22]

Today chaparral is used as mentioned and as an antiseptic for infection. It is also sold in combination herbal formulas that cannot be labeled to state that they treat any particular disorder, such as cancer. The only legally recognized cancer treatments are chemotherapy and radiation; it is against the law to advertise a natural herb or formula as potentially helpful. Cancer patients with systemic lymph gland involvement have only a small chance of living more than five years. Research has not shown that either radiation or chemotherapy is a cure when cancer has spread to other areas of the body. These patients should be free to choose any method they wish to remove the cancer. Those who survive in spite of the odds have been found to be optimists who have used a variety of conventional and alternative health practices. Mind-set was found to be more important than the treatment used!

Echinacea
(Echinacea angustifolia)
Commonly known as purple coneflower, this beautiful flowering plant used to blanket entire fields of the American plains and still grows everywhere herbal companies haven't overpicked it. Its wonder-drug reputation threatens its existence in the wild. For good reason, the Indians used it for everything. It contains natural antibiotic qualities and heals infections. It was used as an antidote for poisonous insects and snakebites and to heal earaches in children and distemper in horses.

Echinacea is commonly stocked in health food sections and stores, and contemporary naturopaths use it in place of antibiotics. In case of severe infection, you should consult your medical doctor, as herbs may not work quickly enough for safety's sake. Use echinacea when you are treating colds, viruses, and minor skin irritations or infections. Using it for minor problems (instead of taking an antibiotic) helps keep your body from becoming immune to prescription antibiotics when you really need them!

This herb, like others, works better in combination. For a cold or flu, use it with vitamin C, goldenseal, wild yam, raspberry tea, and myrrh gum tincture. Myrrh is an Old World herb used in biblical times as a drug and for its perfume. The condensed myrrh sold in tincture form will not smell and taste anything like perfume. It is quite strong and should be used only as directed on the bottle and when you are sick. It may be one of the few herbal drugs that kills viruses. When the commercial companies "discover" its virtues, watch for the price to skyrocket.

Goldenseal

(Hydrastis Canadensis)

This herb is currently almost extinct in the wild but, fortunately, is cultivated commercially. The Indians used it to treat battle wounds and serious contagious venereal diseases brought from Europe. Goldenseal has an affinity for mucous membranes and is used today to treat infections of the teeth and gums, tonsillitis, chronic intestinal disorders, and skin problems. It is another miracle herb containing alkaloids, which means it is strong and powerful and should be used only when needed. Combined with myrrh gum tincture, it is a powerful antiseptic agent that can be used when traveling in places where doctors are not available.

Saint Johns wort

(Hypericum perforatum)

Saint Johns wort, also an antispastic nervine, is included in this section because of its unique constituent, hypericin, which acts as an antidepressant. Even though research demonstrated fifty years ago that it was an antidepressant and it was listed in the *Merck Manual* for doctors, only recently has it begun to be utilized, in place of prescription antidepressants, by people finding out about it and purchasing it over the counter. Saint Johns wort is useful for menstrual cramps, nervousness, insomnia, acne, and liver cleansing.

Like the prescriptive antidepressants, it needs to be taken regularly before effects are noticed. Follow the instructions on the bottle and vary dosage to experiment with your energy level. Remember though, the mind cannot be "cured" if your depression is caused by repressed anger or disappointment, the subject of the next section, which discusses the mind's influence on the body's physical well-being: *The mind is the temple of your spirit.*

HEALING YOUR NERVES WITH HERBS

Catnip

(Nepeta cataria)

Catnip, which is usually associated with cats, grows wild all over America. It is one of the few herbs recommended by physicians for babies, including Humbart Santillo, N.D., author of *Natural Healing with Herbs.* In doses of one tablespoon per one pint of boiling water (steep covered until body temperature), it can be used as a bowel injection for babies with colic or added to baby formula to ease pain. Use in crisis situations only. Adult dosages are three tablespoons per one pint of boiling water; again, don't boil, just steep until body temperature. Use all herbal formulas in moderation and only when needed.

Lady's Slipper

(Cypripedium varieties)

Lady's slipper was used like valerian, which is a distantly related species, for nervous conditions in women and children, especially by Indians in the eastern part of the United States, such as the Cherokee and Ojibwas. The herb, used for menstrual cramps, insomnia and hysteria, is both a sedative and an antispasmodic. Adopted by early white doctors (before pharmaceutical companies), it found its way into popular use for men as well.

Steep several teaspoons in about twelve ounces of water longer than ordinary (up to an hour). The tincture is stronger but easier to use. Take up to thirty drops a day as needed. Combine with lobelia and skullcap for increased relief from cramping or nervous attacks.

Skullcap

(Scutellaria lateriflora)

Another indigenous nervine is skullcap, an antispasmodic and relaxant. Like its friend valerian, it grows in damp places all across the United States.

Skullcap helps promote sleep, reduces agitation, and helps heal frayed nerves. Certain tribes used it in rituals to promote menstruation, to treat such female problems as cramping, and as an aid in breast feeding.

Like other nervines, it soothes a nervous heart. Note: All heart palpitations or similar problems should first be checked by a physician.

Those who are concerned about their sex drive should be aware that the old literature claims nervines will reduce "undue sexual desire!" I guess one has to decide what kind of "tension" one wants and when one wants it. However, because constitutions vary, perhaps nervous personalities might benefit from small doses. Depressive personalities probably won't. Again, try the nervines and see!

Valerian

(Valeriana officinalis)

Valium, a valuable sedative in surgical procedures and at one time a widely overprescribed drug, was derived by synthetically duplicating chemical elements from the herb valerian. Although Valium has since earned a bad reputation, it still is a valuable surgical drug used in countless out-patient operations to temporarily render the person unaware of pain as the doctors work on the body.

Valerian is a multifaceted healer that was used by Native Americans for alleviating nervous symptoms and for easing the pain of swollen joints. Its root was ground into flour to eat in times of famine.

It is indigenous to countries with low lying meadows and wet marshes or riverbanks. It is easily grown in a backyard garden. Cats and rats are said to be as attracted to valerian root as they are to another nervine, catnip. Valerian mixes well with other nerviness such as catnip, skullcap, yellow lady's slipper, or a little lobelia to make a mixture to help you sleep, relax, or be less anxious.

The tincture is easiest to use. Take one dropperful of valerian tincture three or four times a day as needed. Double as an emergency dose for spasms or cramps. It is also available in capsule form. Follow the directions on the label. Do not use valerian daily or indiscriminately. As with all drug treatments, do not use it in place of dealing with the problem causing the nervousness.

Although those who grow valerian may have enough root to place in a hot bath, for those who purchase it, it is too precious to waste. Valerian may be drunk as a tea; pour boiling water over several teaspoons of root until infused.

Valerian, as do all nervines, has a strong taste and smell. Although the herb acts as a relaxant in normal doses for humans, cats become giddy and excited, perhaps because of their small size or different brain systems. For cats, it is an aphrodisiac! For humans, these relaxants may have the

opposite effect, unless you are the obsessive-compulsive type who needs to be less uptight.

Wild Lettuce
(Lactuca species)

A natural nervine, wild lettuce was used by various Native American tribes to treat female disorders and to help with childbirth and breast feeding. A natural sedative, it may have been used in ritual for female "detoxification": to release contamination from menstruation (blood was thought to interfere with the power of the medicine rituals).

Iceberg lettuce, the favorite with Americans, has the fewest minerals and vitamins of all the green leafy vegetables, but has small quantities of sedative-type characteristics. Unfortunately for those liking big, heavy meals, it is thought by some to slow down, and thus interfere with, digestion! Bad news for those steak and potato eaters who thought they were eating enough vegetables with a couple of leaves of iceberg lettuce!

Wild Onions
(Allium mutabile)

Onions were eaten raw, boiled in stews, and fried. They have both antiseptic and decongestant qualities. They aid in digestion, expel worms, and kill bacterial and fungus infections. Onion poultices were used to heal battle wounds and skin infections. Both onions and garlic lower blood pressure. Some people believe onions produce a drowsy feeling similar to taking a nervine or sedative.

Onions when worn, like garlic, were thought to provide protection due to their volatile oils. In *Indian Herbalogy of North America*, Alma Hutchens points out that crushed onion or garlic will kill a bacteria culture in a few minutes when placed next to it. During the Middle Ages, or "vampire season," perhaps the wearing of garlic around the neck actually kept away bacterial invasions or other nasty critters.

 # NATIVE AMERICAN CLEANSING HERBS

It is no accident that the procedures and herbs used today to cleanse the internal body are native to North America and were used by the Indians centuries ago. There are two main reasons for this. First, because contemporary allopathic doctors don't believe in internal cleansing, pharmaceutical allopathic doctors don't see any reason to synthesize natural herbal ingredients as marketable prescription drugs. Second, they work. Thus, ancient herbal remedies are legal, inexpensive, and plentiful, as well as being effective and safe.

Use of herbal remedies requires common sense and moderation as they do contain ingredients that affect the body. For example, the oils and tinctures of wormwood and black walnut are highly potent and concentrated. Follow the instructions on the label, as mixture strengths vary by manufacturer, and be sure to keep them out of the reach of children.

Aloe Vera

(Agave Americana)

Native Americans drank the juice of the plant and used it to heal wounds and abrasions and soothe dry or sunburned skin. Because Americans have abused their digestive tracts and intestines, thousands drink aloe vera juice daily to promote rebuilding of the colon and small intestines, to help heal ulcers, and to use as a gentle laxative.

As the juice is popular, many brands are available. Old favorites include George's Aloe Vera juice and Lily of the Desert juice and gel. The writer prefers the gel for internal cleansing. Avoid brands containing large quantities of preservatives.

Pregnant women should consult their naturopathic physician or medical doctor because of the laxative qualities of the drink, especially women expected to have trouble carrying their babies to full term.

Healthy pregnant women may find the juice helpful for relieving constipation, but should avoid taking it in large quantities during the last trimester.

Cleansing techniques such as colon irrigation, enemas, or hot sweat baths shouldn't be used by pregnant women. Pregnancy is one time you don't want to circulate poisons in the body, even to discharge them. Do your cleansing before you get pregnant. Aloe vera shouldn't be used by people with possible appendicitis or cirrhosis of the liver.

Aloe vera has the added advantage of improving health because it provides carbohydrates and is touted to contain all the essential amino acids. It is believed to help organs and tissues recover from radiation and to help cleanse the liver, spleen, kidney, and bladder. To prevent or expel pinworms in children, mix aloe vera juice with fruit juice or dilute it with warm water to use as an enema.

Black Walnut
(Juglans nigra)
Black walnut, a vermifuge, is one of the herbal foods used by Native Americans to dispel worms in the body.

Black walnut capsules or tincture can be taken during or after a cleansing fast or any time in between. The tincture is liquid and easily absorbed by the body. Take the recommended dosage for the tincture, capsules, or other form you have chosen, as strength varies. Herbal black walnut is a vermifuge because it contains iodine, a strong disinfectant and toxin to putrefaction. For that reason, it should be kept out of the reach of children.

Black walnut has the added advantage of giving the body needed iodine—essential for thyroid functioning. Midwesterners and other groups of people who don't have access to seafood sometimes develop goiters around the Adam's apple, one result of an iodine deficiency. Everyone's thyroid functioning varies; for those who demonstrate hyperthyroidism (a hyperactive thyroid), taking iodine on a daily basis could

cause nervousness, sleeplessness, hair loss, and an overworked heart. This is an individual matter and one that needs assessment from a naturopathic doctor, a person who does muscle testing (kinesiology), or a medical doctor who can administer thyroid tests.

Cascara Sagrada
(Rhamnus purshinana)
The Indians used cascara sagrada, which is the bark of the California buckthorn tree, as a laxative. Even in the medical industry, this herb has wide recognition as a laxative and is included in a number of preparations sold in drugstores. Constipation is at an all-time high. Accordingly, pharmaceutical companies have synthesized ingredients from this herb. It is not recommended for spastic colons but seems to be preferred by those with the opposite problem—lazy or untoned bowels. Personality and body structure go together. Judge your own temperament and choose your laxative accordingly. Interestingly, cascara is thought to increase the production of bile, which would be needed by those not as easily "galled" and perhaps "looser" in gut and temperament than more uptight types.

Castor Oil
Oil from the castor bean is a traditional laxative. It is cultivated extensively in the United States because so many people use it. Do not get in the habit of using this oil as a daily laxative because it depletes the body of vitamins A and E and results in vitamin deficiencies. You can tell those who use it every day: Their skin looks like old leather. Castor oil is useful as a laxative after a heavy purging or fasting and for heated oil packs used on the body, as described earlier.

Senna
(Cassia marilandica)
Native Americans used senna, a cathartic (laxative), to dispel parasites, purge the colon and, perhaps, to help bring on menstruation or

childbirth in unusual circumstances. The bruised root, moistened with water, was used as a dressing for sores and, mixed with water, drunk for sore throats and fevers.

Today senna is combined with fruit leaves or soothing herbs to provide the mildest laxative effects in the bowels. One of the popular senna combinations is sold under the name of Swiss Kriss Tabs and is available in health food stores.

Natural herbal laxatives are a temporary and necessary fix now and then, but they do not clear an impacted colon. That is the purpose of the cleansing diet. Herbal laxatives improve health when used only as needed by keeping material from continuing to gather and lodge in the intestines. People with spastic colons may require sporadic use of mild laxatives as a preventative and should seek medical help or use anti-spasmodic herbs.

Slippery Elm
(Ulmus fulva michx.)
Slippery elm, widely recognized by Native Americans for its soothing, healing effects, was utilized by Indians all across the United States to help heal wounds and to cleanse the body.

Slippery elm comes from the inner bark of the red elm tree. It is slippery and the mucilage is healing and anti-inflammatory. Slippery elm also contains tannins that give it an astringent quality. This combination is good for healing and soothing mucous membranes and the digestive tract.

Today herbologists use slippery elm as an herbal remedy for a variety of digestive disorders, such as duodenal ulcers, colitis, gastritis, diarrhea, and constipation. In diarrhea, it heals irritated membranes and acts as an inner astringent. In severe cases of diarrhea it should be discontinued, as the slippery qualities, useful in constipation, might contribute to dehydration.

Eating onions and garlic provides a natural antibiotic for the body and discourages bacteria and parasites. Sage and wormwood are useful herbal treatments for vermin.

One Native American and naturopathic cure for parasites is to eat one cup of raw pumpkin seeds a day for three days while otherwise eating as little as possible. People with delicate or spastic colons should whirl seeds in their coffee grinders and eat them with cereal or during an apple juice fast. Take some castor oil to speed up the elimination process.

One of the little-known symptoms of parasites in the body is a tendency to have a florid coloring around the nose and cheek area. Other symptoms are itching, fluttering and spasms of the colon, bloating, flatulence, pain, irritability and increased hunger. Sometimes people will dream of having "germs" or unwanted objects in their bodies. All too often the digestive tract is ignored by physicians, yet it contains hundreds of different types of parasites: worms and amoebas ranging in size from those too small to be seen without a microscope to a tape worm, which can grow many feet longer than the human body it inhabits—a creature to rival any Hollywood horror movie! Disbelievers with strong stomachs can use a jeweler's magnifying glass or a microscope to examine suspicious contents expelled from their colon during a fast.

When parasites invade vital organs or other parts of the body, strange symptoms can manifest. Standard medical tests may be diagnostically ineffective. If you suspect the problem, try to find a medical specialist who knows the proper test to give for detection. Routine fecal or urine samples may not find anything because the sample may be clean.

SMUDGING HERBS

For smudging, shamans, of course, always prefer natural or wild varieties for spiritual reasons and for their effectiveness outdoors. The stronger the odor, the better the herb for smudging, thus they favor the non-cultivated varieties. The odor comes from the presence of essential oils in the herbs or plants, which in turn is the main reason for their prized medicinal qualities.

⌘ SAGE

Sage grows wild all over the United States in species ranging from large, rangy, twiggy bushes with tough leaves to small, single-stemmed plants with delicate, silver, velvet-like leaves. Unfortunately for lay people, even herbalists fail to distinguish between the two main unrelated varieties of herbs called sage.

First, there is the sage species (*Artemisia*), commonly known as wormwood, which includes "sage brush" and related species such as *Artemisia vulgaris*, known as mugwort. The *Artemisia* varieties used by Native Americans for centuries are indigenous to America. Included in this family is the silver sage prized by Indians and often called sacred sage. This is a single stemmed plant, about nine inches tall, which grows wild in the desert as well as in temperate climates and at all altitudes. This herb grows prolifically even in poor soil. Healers recognize the male plant as different from the female plant and use each accordingly when treating the different sexes.

Second, there is the sage that is related to the mint family (*Salvia officinalis*) and is commercially cultivated and sold in grocery stores for flavoring foods such as turkey dressing. It has been used by Native Americans for several centuries and grows wild throughout the United States. It, too, has variations within the species and close chemical relatives in other plant groups.

The mint variety is indigenous to Europe but has been in America for several hundred years, perhaps brought by the Spaniards. Sage occupies an important role in European and mid-Eastern herbal history. Today, both species are termed "sage" colloquially because of similar odor and characteristics. To distinguish between the two species, not to mention the varieties within the species, requires an herbologist.

Further complicating identification are the dozens of labels given by local people to the same variety of sage. For example, varieties have been called black sage, purple sage, Texas sage, little sage, women's herb, little herb, lad's love, garden sage, wild sage, blue sage, silver sage, sacred sage, chia sage, squaw-root, absinthe, lyre-leafed sage, scarlet sage, thistle sage,

crimson sage, hummingbird sage, white sage, mugwort, and sage brush.

Reference books contain Indian names for plants that are usually guesses as to which herbs they are. Sage is mentioned frequently, but it is sometimes impossible to identify specific varieties. Other species unrelated to those frequently called sage were also used to treat similar disorders.

The *Artemisia frigida* variety, known as little silver sage or—by this writer—sacred sage, is often called little wild sage. Sioux call it women's medicine, *Wia-ta-pezhe*; Omaha-Ponca tribes called it little gray herb, *Pezhe-hota zhinga*; and *kiwokki* was the term used by Pawnee.[22]

Grocery-store sage won't impress you with its aroma compared to its worthy addition to turkey. Conversely, silver sage is too pungent for dressing but adds a sacred, aromatic touch to your prayers.

Sage brewed for tea should be confined to commercial varieties bought in your health food store, unless you know what you are picking. Try wild sages if you are familiar with them and know they haven't been sprayed. For this reason, avoid sage along highways and roads.

To preserve the herb's existence, do not pick wild sage during droughts or pull it up by the roots. The plants are easily recognized by their pungent odor, one reason fledgling medicine healers and commercial retailers are harvesting it from the wild. Brush sage is more plentiful and is rougher and larger to handle but less endangered. Just dry the sage upside down and then pull leaves off the stems (using gloves), discarding the rest in your compost pile or making a safe outside fire, as branches burn like paper.

Brush sage is sold in stores in bundles for smoldering and consequent smoke. These handheld bundles work well outside. Don't use them inside as sparks are certain to burn holes in your carpet unless you have a large fireproof area where the stick can sit and where you don't mind the smoke. Inside, use incense or smolder your sacred sage in bits or in small sticks in a fireproof receptacle.

Native Americans used wormwood or sagebrush varieties to kill parasites, hence the name. Wormwood essential oil concentrate should be

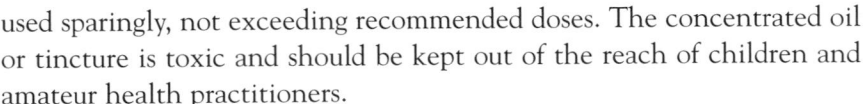

used sparingly, not exceeding recommended doses. The concentrated oil or tincture is toxic and should be kept out of the reach of children and amateur health practitioners.

Because it was available, sage has been used over the years to treat countless ailments and, because of its high oil content, seems to be effective for colds, sore throats, and parasites and as a tea for encouraging sweating and helping digestion. It may also contribute to the health of the sexual glands by clearing congestion of lymph or bodily fluids.

◧ JUNIPER

Juniper, like sage, was a versatile and important vegetation to the ancients and remains so to the present. Although both juniper and sage are chief smudging herbs, they are far too versatile for only that use. Junipers, cedars, and pines contributed countless gifts to native peoples. These trees furnished hardy supplies of vitamins and valuable components for medicine. They are clearly one of the outstanding natural wonders of Earth. With them, Indians healed, bathed, worshipped, gave offerings, smudged people and dwellings, and constructed sacred teepees and lodges. Indians burned dried limbs for warmth and spiritual protection, fashioned branches for fences, and used the needles for bedding and smudging ceremonies.

Berries and needles were administered for treating ailments of every kind. The leaves and berries used for healing accounted for cures, and the berries and pine nuts contributed food. Juniper needles contain high dosages of vitamin C, which, when drunk, helped supplement the lack of fresh fruit in the winter. Juniper berries contain essential oils, tannin, and organic acids. Red Cloud brewed the leaves for drinking and bathing to help his people at the Pine Ridge Indian Reservation. Melvin Gilmore, in *Uses of Plants by the Indians of the Missouri River Region*, notes that Red Cloud found success with this plant during the Asiatic cholera epidemic of 1845–50 and saved some of his people.

Native Americans called juniper "white man's cedar." Confusion of

the two species is reflected in the scientific and popular names. Desert white cedar is actually a member of the juniper family (*Juniperus monosperma*) as is Eastern red cedar (*Juniperus virginia*). Both were used in ceremonial smudging. In California, Western red cedar (*thuja occidentalis*) and California incense cedar (*Libocedrus descurrens*) were used for smudging because they were readily available.

If you ask nurseries for accurate labeling, you probably will find as much confusion as there is for "real smudging wood" among shamans. The reason for different viewpoints is that all the names have been used interchangeably at one time or another, and there is no difference among varieties for use in smudging ceremonies.

These trees also make wonderful additions to your yard as they provide decorative and esthetic additions to your landscaping. If you live in a dry area, make sure you give the plants extra water, and remember that if you are going to plant one in your yard, you want one that will grow only to a size appropriate for the space. You want one that is free of bagworm; check with your plant nursery.

For smudging use, either variety is fine. If you're collecting wood in the forest, choose loose and dried needles, sticks, and limbs. Never cut down healthy juniper branches or trees for smudging purposes. Collect the fallen leaves or weak or crowded branches to dry for burning. A large tree in your yard will drop enough needles in the summer or during a dry spell to provide plenty of smudging material. Dried, these are extremely flammable because of their oils, so they should be stored properly. Do not burn your Christmas tree or large, dried branches in an indoor fireplace, as you might start a fire.

Cedar shavings to use as clearing herbs are sold by both lumberyards and spiritual stores. Juniper and cedar incense is available, as are oils and candles. These are easy to use indoors and give the air a festive aroma. Use at holidays as well as daily to give you and your home a good sensory experience. Sweet grass, pruned rose bushes, and fallen willow sticks make good additions to outdoor smudging and fires.

Preservation of Juniper

Although the traditional red man rarely destroyed the esteemed juniper without need, these trees have been indiscriminately cut down over the years, thereby reducing the supply of their fruit, which is a foodstuff for wild birds and animals. Junipers also provide bird homes and shelter. They traditionally have been used as Christmas trees, and today families in certain regions still go out and cut one to decorate for the holidays.

For those desiring a "real tree," junipers can be purchased from nurseries with their roots balled for replanting. These trees can be kept inside in a warm room for several days before Christmas. Once planted, they must be watered frequently for the next few months to establish a root system, or they will die.

These trees offer dignity and protection to your yard and home as they grow. When planting, be sure to allow enough space for growth. Large-variety juniper trees, given proper care, grow quickly and within ten years will be wider and taller than an average room. Pick young trees that are bushy, for they will grow up to look similar. The cultivated groundcover varieties are beautiful when bagworm-free and used to border driveways or sidewalks.

Using Juniper Today

Herbal companies sell the berries in various forms in health food stores. Juniper has diuretic qualities and is used today for assisting sluggish kidneys or bladder problems. It makes a favorful and nutritious tea. Juniper has stimulating properties and is a healthful replacement for regular tea or coffee. Kidney diseases may be irritated by juniper, so always check with your doctor before treatment of undiagnosed kidney ailments.

Juniper Berry

For bloating, backaches, or water retention caused by sluggish kidneys, take several capsules with water. Crush or blend dried berries in a coffee grinder and brew them in water for a tea, one teaspoon of herbal berries

to one cup boiling water. Never put herbs in a microwave or boil herbs unless directions specify. If you want to use a microwave, first heat the water in the microwave and then remove it and add the herb to steep. Boil mineral or spring water on the stove before adding the herb.

 # SHAMANIC HERBS

Tobacco

Indigenous to the "new world," tobacco was eventually cultivated by Indians. Their cultivation patterns, uncovered by archaeologists excavating ancient Indian sites, help determine early Indian migration and trade routes.[23]

Tobacco originated with Native Americans as an herb used for healing and sacraments. Today, because of widespread addiction and consequent health problems, the consensus is that tobacco is not suitable for daily inhaling. It shouldn't be inhaled or chewed. Unless you are a medicine healer or a pipe carrier, it is best used as a spiritual offering or wrapped in cloth for tiny prayer bundles.

Native American shamans, whose opinions on its use vary, still commonly use tobacco. Some are addicted, yet it doesn't diminish their power. In my experience, modern medicine people use tobacco sparingly or only ceremonially, believing constant use does not attract spirit helpers as it becomes commonplace. Old timers do their work as they were taught and accomplish healing whether they smoke or not. Shamans who aren't addicted use tobacco for pipe ceremonies, to clear their own auras, or to achieve an altered state of consciousness so they can prophesy.

In the pipe ceremony, tobacco may be replaced by or cut with sage, sweet grass, licorice, or any of the herbs mentioned previously. When mixed with other herbs, the pipe contents were called *kinnikinnik*, an Algonquian word meaning "that which is mixed." Rituals often took

place at special times of the month or at a seasonal solstice or equinox. Sage is the favored supplement or replacement for tobacco.

Why do people smoke? There are validated studies showing that smoking improves concentration and memory, even among smokers.[24] One would guess tobacco would have more punch for nonsmokers who use it for increased awareness. Unfortunately, it also pollutes from within and is a major cause of disease.

Nicotine, like caffeine, is one of the most addictive substances known. It affects brain-wave function, alters mood, and serves as a biological reward (physically and mentally rewarding) for humans and laboratory animals. People with addictions to these substances have to increase the dosages to get the same effect and suffer withdrawal if they don't continue use. Too much caffeine brings on anxiety and eventually cancels out increased clarity. Try skipping your morning coffee and you get a headache or diminished mental acuity. Add an extra cup when needed (not daily) and receive extra thinking power (provided you aren't drinking too much to begin with).

Tobacco achieved success as a healing aid because it was used only when needed. Remember, there were no painkillers, synthetic morphine, or pharmacies in early America. Original tobacco was strong, and Native Americans used it to discharge mucous and dilate congested lungs, bronchial tubes, and ear canals.

Nicotine contains norepinephrine, which dilates mucous membranes, speeds heart rate, and stimulates the adrenal gland. In a severely ill patient, without modern antibiotics, the tobacco might have prevented congestive heart failure for patients with fluid in the lungs. Morphine, quinine, codeine, nicotine, caffeine, mescaline, and lobaline are all part of a diverse nitrogen-containing substance family produced by plants known as alkaloids. They are all used today in standard contemporary medical practice, as well as by shamans.

Because tobacco has concentrated alkaloids, Native Americans used it as a disinfectant to treat wounds. It was also used to relieve pain. In

early medicine, datura (*Datura stramonium* or "jimson weed") and sage (and/or tobacco) were used as a smoking mixture for asthma and tuberculosis and no doubt provided some type of relief.

For religious use, tobacco was ingested or drunk as tea with datura (to induce vomiting for purifying before a ceremony). Tobacco and datura are poisonous when ingested.

Jimson weed is called "locoweed" by farmers familiar with the effects on their cattle after eating it. Overdoses from datura ingestion in people trying to have hallucinations have resulted in deaths and account for admission of an increased number of teenagers to emergency rooms. Chemical companies today use concentrated ingredients from nicotine to make a powerful insecticide, but nicotine is also added to pharmaceutical drugs to increase their effect.

Children should not be around tobacco smoke due to the effects of secondhand smoke. Habitual breathing of second-hand tobacco smoke creates toxic levels of nicotine and tar (creosote) in the lungs. If that isn't enough, contemporary cigarettes also contain saltpeter, formaldehyde, and other chemicals that cause disease and impotence.

For shamans and smokers, the Santa Fe Natural Tobacco Co. in Santa Fe, New Mexico, has a variety of natural and organic tobaccos, as well as sage sticks and herbal blends. Regular tobacco companies are beginning to offer their version of "pure tobacco." Pregnant women shouldn't smoke tobacco or use herbs unless their use is prescribed by a medical doctors or certified natural health practitioner.

Gentian, myrtle, magnolia, slippery elm, and the nervines are reported to help those trying to break the nicotine habit. These herbs can be taken in capsules or drunk as a tea. Gentian root is chewed at intervals as needed.

Sage

While sage is second to tobacco as *the* prized sacred offering, it is *first* for versatility and health benefits. Sage has been discussed on page 128 because it ranks first today as a clearing herb for smudging.

Lobelia

(Lobelia inflata)

Lobelia was called Indian Tobacco by early settlers who observed its use among Native Americans. Seminole and Creek tribes of Oklahoma (after translocation) called it Little Tobacco, or Old Man's Tobacco. Indians believed it had spiritual and magical qualities and used it ceremonially. Today naturopathic healers call it the "herb with a brain" for its quality of enhancing the effectiveness of other herbs when used in combination with them.

Chemically, lobelia resembles tobacco in that both contain alkaloids (lobaline in lobelia, nicotine in tobacco) and are strong taken in quantity (a little goes a long way). Both herbs stimulate in small doses and act as relaxants in large doses. If you take too much, both are emetics (cause vomiting). In appearance, the lobelia plant resembles tobacco but is only about ten inches high.

Lobelia is a highly effective and versatile herb and has been used for internal and external healing for varied health problems. In previous centuries it was used to treat serious diseases and its scientific name, *siphilitica*, denotes the disease. According to the literature of the time, Native Americans used lobelia to cure syphilis and gonorrhea brought over by the Europeans. It is considered to be a powerful herb with strong narcotic properties.

Michael Weiner, in his book *Earth Medicine Earth Food*, notes that, as had been rumored by Native American healers, European physicians did not obtain the cure for the venereal disease. Listed as possible reasons for the success Indians had with treatment were the facts that they used the herb fresh as opposed to dried and administered it in combination with other herbs, such as the bark of the wild cherry tree. Physicians didn't consider better health practices and spiritual application as variables.

Eaten fresh in large quantities it is poisonous to livestock, and large doses may render a person immobile or unconscious. Theoretically,

people wouldn't eat the plant raw and, if they did, would vomit before they reached lethal doses. Lobelia might be the drug used by Voodoo doctors to render cursed people into a zombie state. Needless to say, if the herb doesn't kill them, the shock of their condition might.

Lobelia is best and most safely taken in small quantities to increase the effectiveness of another herb. Unfortunately, the FDA declared it illegal to sell lobelia in combination with another herb, but you can still buy it alone and combine it with other herbs for remedies.

Lobelia is expensive, but a little goes a long way. It is used currently for lung problems such as asthma and in combination with other herbs, such as mullein, for respiratory ailments. It works with nervines such as valerian or skullcap for anxiety and appears to enhance the efficiency of other herbal remedies if added in small doses. Use one capsule or one-half dropper (about ten drops) of lobelia tincture with another herbal mixture if applicable.

An entry by seventeenth century French cleric, Father Julien Binneteau, in his Journal of a Voyage to North America reveals a glimpse of the European missionary point of view, and an example of the clash in ideologies between their strict Christian beliefs and the practices of the Native American tribes.

God continues to be served here, in spite of the opposition of the devil. In public they perform a hundred mummeries full of impiety; and talk to the skins of animals, and to dead birds, as divinities. They claim that medicinal herbs are gods, from whom they have life, and that no others be worshipped. Every day they sing songs in honor of their little manitous, as they call them. They inveigh against our religion and against the missionaries.[25]

Chapter Six

SPIRIT

American natives had a rich cosmological mythology. However, students of Native American religion believe the term mythology is misleading, due to the similarities in traditional sacred beliefs with those of other major religions of the world, including Christianity. Although authorities disagree, Indian tribes conceived a central power source translated in English as the Great Spirit. This divine spiritual essence shaped and evolved the universe into form.

COSMOLOGY

Wakan Tanka as Grandfather is the Great Spirit independent of manifestation, unqualified, unlimited, identical to the Christian Godhead or to the Hindu *Brahma-Nirguna. Wakan Takan* as Father is the Great Spirit considered in relation to His manifestation, either as Creator, Preserver, or Destroyer, identical to the Christian God, or to the Hindu *Brahma-Saguna...* Earth is considered under two aspects, that of Mother and Grandmother. *The former is the earth considered as the producer of all growing forms, in act; whereas Grandmother refers to the ground or substance of all growing things— potentiality.*[26]

Whether the different spirit forms are the One Power in varying representations, or an army of distinctly separate lesser spirits much like the Christian angels, is in dispute. Wak Ka Tah, Wakan, Wakan Tanka, or Wakonda—names for the Great Spirit in different Indian languages—is the conceptualization of God as a vast universal power. The question is whether this is a deity with the ability to manifest in different forms, or

a single, powerful energy or entity ruling over lesser spirit helpers in animal, natural, or humanlike form. We will never know the original Native American concept of the Great Spirit, due to four hundred years or so of Christian missionary efforts. Although they were not completely successful in washing the concept out of the Indian consciousness, they effectively diluted it. Other ancient religions considered God to manifest in various forms as well as to be formless and invisible. One thing is certain: The Native American conceptualization of God was not limited to a human, manlike image.

Native Americans believed powerful spirits created and shaped the world. In Indian mythology, supernatural creators of the world were a divine energy. The divine essences, such as animal or nature beings, shifted at will from one form to another, to heal, to teach lessons, or to mold the heavens. These shape-shifting beings always were considered to be in spirit form, not actual animals or climatic conditions.

It was believed power could reside in any natural object. All living things had life both visible and invisible. Plants were part of the same kingdom as people. Both shared a consciousness and had power. Any natural object, animate or inanimate, had an essence that could be described as a soul or life force.

Other great religions emphasize the concept that all substances from the earth originated and developed from a universal life force. Anaxagoras, a Greek, designated the Nous or the Animating Soul as present in every atom. Helena P. Blavatasky, author of *The Secret Doctrine*, noted "the conception of a general Spirit-Soul pervading all Nature is the oldest of all philosophical notions."

Native Americans didn't see the world in hierarchical fashion, with the spirits ranked from the highest to the lowest according to a power structure. However, the One God or Great Spirit was generally considered unavailable for assisting in mundane earthly affairs. Semi-divine spirits such as Corn Maiden and Rain Maker existed to respond to prayers for help from those on Earth.

The Navajo are an exception. According to Harold Driver, author of *Indians of North America*, the Navajo believed the dominant leader of the world creators to be Changing Woman. She created humans and helped teach them how to control the forces of nature. "Second in importance to Changing Woman is her husband the Sun.... Third in rank are the Hero Twins, Monster Slayer and Child of the Water.... Of lesser importance are First Man and First Woman. First Man was creator of the universe." There were several groups of lesser spirits, which included Coyote and Thunder People.

Changing Woman was the only holy personality who was always helpful to humans. All the others switched at will into fearful creatures such as tricksters or witches.

SACRED HERBS

Sacred herbs, smoked in a pipe or offered as prayer bundles, helped the medicine man to achieve an altered state of consciousness. It was a sacrament that represented honor and hopefully delivered "grace" if offered in a humble manner by a spiritual person. The holy man or woman left his or her body to perform miracles or visit distance places.

The pipe was sacred and was used unsmoked as a symbol. Tobacco and other sacred herbs were offered through the pipe as symbols of the benefits derived from spiritual helpers sustaining life and grace; it represented gratitude for help received. Promises made with the pipe represented the highest integrity and were considered binding—never to be broken.

The pipe served as a sacred tool for ritualistic offerings through the shaman's body as it represented his people. The term *pipe holder* is reserved for those individuals with the ability to have special religious powers considered honorable enough to use and smoke sacred herbal offerings.

Praying with the Sacred Pipe after offering it to the four directions, heaven and earth, is done by a considerable number of

Lakota people. This is the common use of the Pipe not reserved to the specialist, that is, the medicine or yuwipi man. This is the way I pray with the Pipe. The Pipe is always filled with tobacco and sealed with sage. In a simple prayer the Pipe is usually not smoked. Individual Lakota pray privately in this manner out of personal devotion and on public occasions as a prayer of thanksgiving or petition.[27]

As described by the Native American Holy Woman, the White Buffalo Maiden, the pipe is a sacred symbolic representation of Earth, a sacred entity, the Mother and Grandmother. The pipe was to be used in prayer and respect for Earth. The carving in the stone of the pipe was of the buffalo calf, a symbol for all the animals of the earth. The wooden stem represented the plants and trees.[28]

Leaving Earth to travel to distant galaxies and spiritual planes enabled the prophet to gather information useful for survival, such as how to provide adequate food supplies and handle four-legged enemies. Medicine men and woman experienced great prophetic dreams and visions during such ceremonies, entering a dimension where physical time and space do not exist. Religious leaders around the world increasingly believe communication beyond the ordinary realms is possible. Today the American Indian Church is legally sanctioned to use peyote in ceremonies to promote visions.

◰ HERBAL SPIRITS

Plants and foodstuff, considered to have spirits or souls blessed their fellow beings, the humans. The kingdom of plants vibrated and pulsated with living energy and awareness. Considered as powerful as animal and nature spirits, they were accorded respect. Humble requests and prayers given during sacred herb sacraments impressed the plant beings and assured cooperation in the future. The traditional Native American handled plants with care, cognizant of plant feelings and emotions. They

believed that plant spirits reacted beneficially when pleased and refused to heal or assist when insulted.

Interestingly, the plant spirits preferred plant offerings like tobacco, lobelia, and sage over mineral or animal dedications. Tobacco, because of its preferred status by the Beings and its own powerful Plant Spirit, was held in the highest regard and status.

Great Spirit helpers attracted to sage or tobacco offerings granted requests from the shaman. Native American leaders used ritual and prayer to offer spiritual herbs before healing commenced, during ceremonies, and for appreciation of help received.

Native Americans didn't distinguish between the healing characteristics or spiritual aspects of a plant because, without favor from the particular Being, the chemical properties of the herb were ineffective.

> If, in truth, you make good offerings of tobacco to your plants, if you give many feasts in their honor, and if you then ask your medicines to put forth their strength, and if, in addition, you talk to them like human beings, then most certainly will these plants do for you what you ask. —A Winnebago Indian[29]

During pipe ceremonies, tobacco or sage didn't have to be smoked personally or burned for smoke. It was presented in prayer bundles, given as a healing herb, presented as a sacred gift in the form of incense, laid on altars, or buried in the ground as a gift to Mother Earth. Indians believed Plant Beings enjoyed food and other treats as well. Earlier, natives enjoying their own harvests (not government rations) routinely included the Plant Beings at their meals, always giving them their own portions.

The first step in religious ceremony was the offering of sacred plants, which displayed respect and good will toward such higher spiritual forces as Earthmother. Religions around the world offer sacred herbs in religious ceremonies. Lighting incense or candles or leaving gifts at

altars in churches and cathedrals have been universal practices throughout history.

Sacred herbs also purified the shaman, the patient and the surrounding environment. In short, using the leaves of certain plants and trees occupied an important role in Indian society and still does to this day.

For modern-day Native Americans and Anglo-Americans interested in the practice of traditional Indian ritual and culture, the purchasing of tobacco or sage for offerings during ceremony is *de rigueur*. Included in a shaman's medicine bundle to this day, tobacco is still considered appropriate as part of your payment for traditional Native American medicine. A healer also appreciates money, meat and needed supplies. The few remaining traditional medicine men and women are not wealthy. Modern shamans will specify an amount to pay for each service.

Habitual daily tobacco smoking by Native Americans didn't occur until traditional ceremonial procedures lessened or became forbidden, or until supplies became plentiful enough for physical addictions to develop.

Daily use of tobacco violated sacred pipe rituals and displayed a lack of respect to the plant spirits who could affect the welfare of the tribe by refusing to give valuable information for survival and well-being. Shamans today believe that smoking sacred herbs daily doesn't attract Indian spirits, but rather repels valuable guidance, as the practice becomes commonplace instead of religious.

Originally, tobacco was mixed with sage, sweet grass, red willow, licorice, marjoram or other pleasant-smelling or -tasting herbs to make the smoke or calumet have a milder taste and to save tobacco supplies. Natural indigenous tobacco was strong and used sparingly. Less sacred herbs, perhaps mixed with tobacco, were smoked in corn husks, black jack leaves and later in reeds and pipes. Among these herbs were angelica, bearberry, mullein, sweet flag root, sweet grass, sumac and corn silk.

FINDING YOUR POWER ANIMAL

An important milestone in the life of many Native American children was the seeking out of their power animal. Among some tribes, this was done during a vision quest. Among others, the power animal revealed itself during a dream or ritual. The power animal appeared because someone asked for it, unlike other spirit helpers who appeared spontaneously. Unless a person was a shaman, there was a need to ask the power animal to reveal itself. Power animals often approached shamans to reveal hidden powers that they possessed and would use in the future.

The power animal was used for protection, power, and for practical purposes such as locating game or giving assistance. To be without a power animal lowered one's self-esteem and status.

Michael Harner, in *The Way of the Shaman*, points out that the shaman recognized the connectedness between humans and animals. "Through his guardian spirit or power animal, the shaman connects with the power of the animal world. . . . The guardian spirit is sometimes referred to by Native Americans as the power animal. . . . It emphasizes the power-giving aspect of the guardian spirit as well as the frequency with which it is perceived as an animal."

Today the power animal is considered a type of guardian angel. Whether the angel is in animal spirit form or is a human teacher in animal guise is unknown. The Native Americans were not concerned with placing their power animals in categories. To always seek the highest aims and goals in using one's power animal assures him a noble guardian.

Power animals are those who are either close to crossing over the Rainbow Bridge or who have crossed it. The Rainbow Bridge is the place of crossing from physical life to the spirit world. It is to the animals what the astral plane is to humans. Those power animals desiring to cross over toward human evolution seek out experiences that will be of service to humans. This boosts their evolution.

Guardian angels that already have crossed the Rainbow Bridge can choose the form in which they will appear. They may appear as animal, bird, or human. The higher teachers who appear as animals are rarely found in the animal whose shape they have assumed. They appear in the form most appropriate for the person and his or her environment.

There are many levels of spiritual attainment in animals, just as there are in humans. They draw from their own experiences and from former evolutions, always seeking higher planes. Guardian angels seek to serve you in any way they can. However, the animal guardians are limited to the physical plane and to practical matters and the teacher guardians are interested in more esoteric questions and issues. Ideally, one needs a variety of guardian angels with as many different skills as possible.

Animal guardian angels like to care for pets and homes. They furnish totems and items representing power and protection. They like to find lost items, heal physical wounds, and help take care of pets and plants. They will guard your car and home and keep unwanted energies and problems away. Sometimes they appear to issue a "wake-up call" or increase your awareness of what is happening around you.

Just as you need different guardian angels, you also need different power animals. Your first power animal is the most important and should complement your personality. Additional power animals will represent different attributes and qualities, providing you with helpers with varied talents. You always will be in control of your power animals and they always will be helpful. If you decide not to use their services, they will drift off and seek others to serve.

⊟ DREAMING YOUR POWER ANIMAL

It is necessary to get into the habit of remembering your dreams before you ask your power animal to visit you. Otherwise, an important contact might not be remembered. To get in this habit, start a dream journal. Set it and a pen by your bed close to an easily turned on lamp. Lamps can be fitted with an attachment so that they turn on when you touch them with your hand. This is handy in the dark and requires less effort.

Set your alarm for one to two hours before you ordinarily wake up. This is the time you do your deepest and most meaningful dreaming, for you are in a delta brain-wave state. Alcohol and central nervous system depressants interfere with reaching this state, so none should be consumed at least several nights before you wish to remember a dream.

Should you be dreaming when the alarm sounds, record your dream in your notebook before getting out of bed. Any activity will interfere with your remembering the dream. After recording it, go back to sleep, after setting your alarm if you have to get up at a certain time.

In the morning, analyze your dream content for messages. Sometimes, your first contact with spirits will provide you with an important message that you will not want to miss. In addition, you will receive important messages that portend the future. Pay careful attention to these dreams because they will give you valuable information. Write down your dreams on a regular basis. After a while it will not be necessary to set your alarm early because your unconscious will get into the habit of releasing material, and you will remember dreams upon awakening.

Before going to bed, look around the house at all the pictures, figurines, and other representations of animals you have around you, including jewelry and slogans on shirts. Browse through pictures and books of animals. Watch for programs or movies that seem to appear at about the time you are interested in contacting your power animal. Do not entertain any previously conceived notions about the identity of your first animal, because this could ruin your experience. Have a totally open mind and an intense desire to learn.

As you prepare for bed, repeat the statement to yourself of your need for a power animal guardian angel. Ask it to appear in your dream. Request that it tell you how it will help you. Ask for its appearance as you drift off to sleep. Do this for as many nights as is necessary to have your dream.

If you need extra assistance, then purchase a deck of animal cards, medicine cards, or a book with animal pictures. Do not use cards or pictures of domestic animals. They cannot be power animals. Native Americans believe that animals tamed by humans have lost their spiritual power base. Before you go to sleep, hold each card or picture up to your face, making sure that the name or picture faces away from you. Go through the assortment until you have a warm feeling when one of the pictures is next to your face. Repeat the process and see if the same picture or pictures give you a sensation of warmth or interest. Narrow down your choices until you select one card or picture.

Before going to bed, take this animal picture and talk to it. "You have a special interest in my welfare. You may not be my power animal but you can help me find it. I will look at you now with intense desire for your help (stare at picture). I can imagine touching you and talking with you. Thank you for your help. Now, I will go to sleep, knowing that I have a helper."

Remove all preconceived ideas as to which animal would be a good advisor or power animal. As in all spiritual contact, you must let go to "let it happen" or it won't. You must be prepared to receive information that you may not want to hear. Fear also will block the experience. If you are afraid, then wait before pursuing your power animal. You can do it later or never; it is your decision. Resistance is a common reaction to discovery. This is readily overcome when a person makes up his or her mind he or she is ready for the experience.

◧ ANIMAL ANALYSIS

If an animal appears to you in a dream, it is significant and it may be your power animal. If it was angry or bared its teeth or fangs, it is not your guide. Also, insects cannot be power animals. If the dream was especially vivid and "felt right," then you have found your animal or bird. Remember, your first animal guide is the most significant because it tells you the most important deficiency in your personality. The type of animal that you dream complements your personality, showing you the quality you most need to cultivate. The following chart will give you some ideas as to why your particular spirit bird or animal has appeared.

Bird/Animal	Type & Interpretation
Badger	Someone is pushing you and you are not fighting back.
Bear	You are a natural helper and person with power but you are not using these qualities.
Beaver	Get your lazy bones going to complete that important project.
Buffalo	Leadership is your hidden talent but it needs developing.
Coyote	You need more fun in your life.
Crow	You will need help in discovering a betrayal.
Deer	You have a need for beauty and gentleness in your life. Let others have control for awhile.
Dolphin/Whale	Expand your awareness beyond your home and self. Community concerns need your attention.
Eagle/Hawk	You are being guided by higher spiritual forces. Important lessons and growth will happen to you.
Elephant	Your mental capabilities are keen but neglected. Neglect the physical for awhile in order to develop your mind.
Fox	You need to get more wily and lose you naiveté.
Frog/Lizard	Your experiences are too mundane. Expand your awareness to include the occult and spiritual.
Horse	Your personal freedom is being suppressed. Letting loose and taking risks are important.
Large Cats	Strength and persistence are needed to accomplish goals.

Moose/Elk	You need more contact with the opposite sex for a better balance of male/female energies.
Mouse	The quietness and non-intrusive qualities of the mouse will give you knowledge that is impossible to see right now because of a tendency to talk rather than obtain insight.
Owl	You have tremendous psychic potential that you have not developed.
Raccoon	You need to get organized and also have more fun.
Ram	Seek spiritual instead of material pleasures.
Sea Gull	You lock yourself into old patterns and routines. Take risks to break out of them.
Skunk	You need more protection and defenses.
Snake	Old and ancient wisdom is yours—unused knowledge is sinful. May also indicate untapped sexuality.
Songbird	Beauty and aesthetics are missing in your life.
Turtle/Tortoise	Patience is absolutely necessary at this time. Slow down.
Wild Hare	Take time to be gentle and to smell the roses.
Wolf	Family needs are being neglected for matters not as important.

Additional power animals may be acquired later. It is unlikely that they will complement your personality to the extent that your first one will. However, they will provide help and skills needed by you during those times. Power animals come and go depending upon the extent to which their help is used. Future animal helpers are acquired in the same manner as the first—you must ask for them.

◲ FINDING YOUR POWER ANIMAL THROUGH IMAGERY

Another method of finding your animal spirit guide is to take your vision quest through imagery. Dr. Michael Harner was the first to write about vision quest imagery, which he adapted from a ritual of the Jivaro people of Peru and Ecuador. The imagery quest is surprisingly easy for most people. Drumming is used as a device to assist in achieving the necessary trance state. Research suggests that drumming puts one quickly into a theta brain-wave state, thus facilitating visions.

Dr. Harner does not like to give too many specifics or suggestions for those attempting their first journey, because he believes that it influences the findings and makes them less individualized. Option One for finding your animal, listed below, follows this philosophy. It is important to avoid disturbing a person while he or she journeys, as it could cause some soul loss. Soul loss occurs when a part of our essence or being remains in another place even though our physical body returns.

Eileen Nauman, a Cherokee Metis, prefers specific information for those journeying as it pertains to the animal selection, such as that discussed in Option Two of finding your animal.

While you are making your imagery journey you should be accompanied by a friend vigorously playing a drum or by an audiocassette of shamanic drumming. Ideally, the drum should be of sufficient quality to give a loud deep sound. Tell the friend to drum briskly for fifteen minutes, then signal the beginning of your return back with seven rapid beats followed by a pause (repeated four times), and then increase the speed of the drumming for several minutes during your return. This rapid beat signals your return from the underworld to the middle world where you live. Your completed return is accompanied by the drummer again beating seven rapid beats and pausing (four times) at the end.

All journeys are best taken in a darkened room or with a covering over your eyes to block light. Recline on the floor (using pillows if you wish) and wear comfortable clothing so there will be as few distractions as possible.

Read the following instructions for your journey and be sure to remember the main points. Use only one option each time you search for a power animal.

⊟ GETTING TO THE LOWERWORLD

I want you to think of an opening that extends down into the earth, such as a cave, a natural spring, or an animal hole in a tree or the ground. The hole becomes large enough for you to enter and you do so, continuing to go down, farther and farther. You go down and down and down. You will be able to smell and feel vividly as you see yourself journeying. Eventually, you will emerge from the opening. You are now in the Lowerworld, where your guardian spirit or power animal is waiting for you. Be aware of the sights, sounds, and smells of the landscape around you. Touch something if you like. (This process will take much longer than it seems here.)

⊟ CHOOSING YOUR ANIMAL

Option One: Keep requesting your power animal to appear until it does. It will have to appear several times to indicate its dedication to you. You cannot choose an insect, or any fish, reptile, or animal with fangs or bared teeth. After finding your power animal (no dialogue is necessary), you may bring the animal out with you or leave it in the Lowerworld. The latter is recommended for your first power animal retrieval.

Option Two: This method is recommended for those experienced in achieving imagery or trance states or those who already have done a power animal retrieval. (The dialogue is easier to handle and less likely to influence or interfere with your vision.)

Soon you will see animals around you. If you do not see any, ask your power animal to appear. Be firm in repeating your request that your animal reveal itself to you. If the animal is on your left side, walk on by. If it comes up behind you, walk way. The only animals that can come from those directions are creatures such as gophers or snakes. If the animal is in front of you or on your right side, it may be your ally. It must either have black, shiny eyes, gold, sparkling eyes, or red eyes. Red eyes are indicative

of older primeval allies. Any other color will be unsatisfactory.

You should ask the animal three questions.
1. What is your name?
2. Will you obey every instruction I give you?
3. How will you help me improve myself?

If the answers to all three questions are satisfactory, turn your back and walk away. The animal must reveal itself to you several more times before you can be sure of its use to you. (When the original animal appears again, it may come from any side.) If the answers to any of the questions are unsatisfactory, thank the animal for coming, but say that you are not interested in it at this time. Be firm in order to make it leave.

If the animal appears to you several more times, you may leave the Lowerworld with it. Be sure that you close the door to the Lowerworld behind you so that no other animal will follow you out. You will come back up the path and exit from the hole or cave where you entered.

Do not be discouraged if you do not find your power animal on your first attempt. Sometimes it takes several journeys before you make contact. With practice, you will find it easy to take a journey whenever you like! Be sure to write down the results of your journey.

ANIMAL SPIRIT COMMUNICATION

Developing communication with animal and bird spirits takes time, dedication, and patience. New attitudes and behaviors are required and there are no definite ways to assess your progress. Many experiences cannot be defined or put into categories. You must develop your intuition and perceptions as you gain experience in order to help you interpret events. Beginning to develop skills of communication with bird and animal spirits is an ongoing lifetime process with no definite answers.

Certain attitudes are needed to help you gain the attention and cooperation of your animal spirit friends. You will have to adapt four behaviors before beginning such communication, however.

1. Love and reverence for all living things.
2. Sincerity of motive and higher purpose.
3. Intense desire for spirit communication.
4. Follow a program to attract and help the bird and animal kingdom.

Respect for all living things and for the ways that they are connected is essential to attracting animals and animal spirits. This includes a knowledge of your own existence as a divine being. You must be aware of and appreciate the sacredness of nature and all her plants and creatures. This understanding is a prerequisite to any meaningful animal communication.

You, no doubt, already have this quality because you are reading this book. This quality is a feeling of love and empathy for all living things which is demonstrated when you attend an animal in distress, nurture a plant or pet, or take interest in the preservation and survival of animal and plant species on our planet.

The most important requirement is sincerity of motive and high spiritual purpose. Motive is everything. The same behavior with varying motives will bring completely different results. Always entertain the highest aims for all concerned in your goals and experiences in life. You can help obtain this difficult attribute by eliminating all doubts, fears, and angers from your thinking. Think positively and always for the good of all. Time is required to bring you to this ideal state of mind. Patience is necessary to change thought patterns and to receive help from the spiritual dimension because linear time does not exist on that plane.

The higher level animal and bird spirits are attracted to your appreciation and interest. Your intense desire acts as a powerful beam radiating outward into your environment. Wish for them and they will come to you. Spend time outside observing nature to help increase both the intensity of your desire and the spirits' availability. Living in the city makes it somewhat more difficult to have your friends visit, but they will find you anyway.

The fourth requirement for attracting your spirit helpers is to be helpful to them. The Native Americans were cognizant of this reciprocal

interaction. They left small offerings of food or charms to be helpful to their spirit and animal helpers. Expand your appreciation of nature to include service and action, and they will come to you in gratitude.

 ## ATTRACTING BIRD AND ANIMAL SPIRIT HELPERS

1. Spend some time outdoors taking in the essence of nature, every day when possible. Walk around a park or the countryside. In inclement weather, drive around and park in a scenic location. Always do this alone so you can begin to sense what nature has to offer. This must be done in silence and solitude. When not possible, gaze out of an open window and focus on plants, trees, and birds. You will be amazed at what you can see outside your window.

2. Buy a bird feeder and position it to be seen when you look outside. Include some food for other animals on the ground.

3. Plant trees and shrubs that attract birds and animals. For example, a female pyracantha bush will attract a mockingbird as a permanent resident, which will give you many delightful moments.

4. If you want a pet, adopt either an animal at the pound òr one being given away in the newspaper. Do not set out to buy a pedigreed animal or buy one impulsively in a pet store. However, if an opportunity for any pet comes along and it feels right, take it, because it may be a special friend.

5. Avoid the purchase of any product or chemical that is tested on animals. Buy natural cosmetics and toiletries that specify no animal testing. The best policy is to avoid purchasing most chemicals, poisons, drugs, insecticides, commercial fertilizers, herbicides, pesticides, and all possible environmental pollutants.

6. Subscribe to a magazine that promotes animal welfare or ecology. Join

an organization that is lobbying or working toward the improvement of conditions for animals, animal rights, or animal and plant habitats.

7. Volunteer to help at the zoo or with groups that preserve wildlife, or join "living" organizations that provide alternatives to euthanasia.

8. Avoid the use of plastics and styrofoam, as they are nonbiodegradable and endanger the environment. Recycle paper and buy recycled goods.

9. Avoid products that use fluorocarbon propellants, which damage the ozone layer of the earth's atmosphere.

10. Eat foods that require lower amounts of energy to be produced, such as grains and vegetables. Animal products require a great deal of energy in their production.

Basically, any action taken by you to preserve or care for nature and her inhabitants will increase your spiritual consciousness and bring you many blessings. This new ecological awareness and action will send messages to the animal and bird spirits and tell them that you are ready to receive their assistance. Any task you take to protect your animal friends will be rewarded many times over. They will be attracted to you and begin to give you many rich experiences. The more interest and concern you show for them, the more help they will give you.

Interpreting Animal Manifestations

Animal spirits communicate with us in many different ways and it is not always possible to distinguish among them. Ordinary animals, insects, and birds may be drawn to you by a vibration field surrounding your body. Song birds are drawn to yards with good vibrations. A friendly neighborhood dog will give you feedback about the warmth of your personality. Bumblebees or angry dogs give you different information. Basically, when insects, birds, or animals are around, they reflect the conditions present in your environment. These animals are not in spirit form, but they are sensitive to your magnetic field and are drawn to you for a reason. Use them as a barometer to assess yourself and your current environmental conditions.

Birds and animals from different dimensions or in spiritual forms may give you warnings or assistance. For instance, crows, hawks, and owls portend the future and are valuable assistants. Of course, the number of birds involved and the activities in which they are engaged are important in the interpretation. A single crow approaching you in unusual fashion may be a warning of a disappointment or a betrayal. But a group of crows chatting merrily in your tree may give you a sign of a friendly gathering that you will join.

If a person in your family is sick, an owl may portend a long illness or his or her death. If you are starting a project, seeing an owl may signal changes ahead or be a warning of a difficult time ahead.

Higher teachers may appear as birds or animals and offer experiences or lessons that provide information or guidance. When this happens, they appear in a form that is acceptable to the person and will avoid arousing suspicion. For example, a bear would not appear to you in the city. Birds and dogs are the most common form of higher spirit intervention. However, these experiences are rare and will not happen until a person has achieved the status of an adept.

Native Americans made no attempt at grouping their spirits in hierarchical form except for the Great Spirits, who were seen as the highest form of intelligence.

The following birds and animals are listed with suggested messages only as a guideline for you. Most important is the context in which they are seen or heard. Notice the rarity of the animal and its description, the activity of the animal, the number of birds or animals involved, its condition, the location, and its proximity and interaction with you. After these considerations, messages are to be interpreted with the personal context of each individual and his or her life's situation.

Animal	Message
antelope	action
armadillo	defended
badger	aggressive
bat	macabre
bear	strength
beaver	accomplishment
beetle	hidden knowing
bighorn sheep	conqueror
blue jay	pushy
bluebird	happiness
buffalo	strength
bull/stallion	sexual energy
burro/donkey	helpful
butterfly	friendly
camel	ornery
canary	joy

ANIMAL	MESSAGE
cat	independent
chameleon	adaptable
chickadee	optimism
chicken	foolish
cockroach	lowest
cow	docile
coyote	cunning
cricket	disharmony
crow/raven	portent
deer	loveliness
dog	loyalty
domestic goose	quarrelsome
domestic sheep	follower
eagle	highest power
elephant	old memory
elk	brave
flamingo	grace
fly	parasitic
frog	sorcery
goat	friendly
hawk	opportunity
heron	spiritual
hummingbird	joy
lark	weather
lizard/toad	old wisdom

ANIMAL	MESSAGE
llama	practical
lynx	psychic
magpie	knowledge
meadowlark	protective
mockingbird	imitative
mole	lack foresight
moose	pride
mountain lion/ cougar	leader
mouse	busy
mule	stubborn
ostrich	stubborn
otter	playful
owl	diviner
parrot	playful
peacock	ostentatious
pelican	saver
pig	intelligence
pigeon in air	mission
pigeon on ground	inertia
porcupine	protected
porpoise/dolphin	teachers
possum	avoidance
quail	family
rabbit	gentle

Animal	Message
raccoon	enterprising
racehorse	high strung
rat	survivalist
red bird/cardinal	beauty
red-headed woodpecker	resourceful
roadrunner	traveler
robin	balance
sea gull	freedom
shark	killer
skunk	defended
snake	challenger
snow goose	fidelity
sparrows	ordinary
spider	deceit
squirrel	resourceful
sturgeon	dominant
turkey	forgetful
turtle/tortoise	old wisdom
whale	universal mind
wild duck	adventure
wild horse	freedom
wild pheasant/ turkey	quick
wolf	organizer
workhorse	plodding

Animal Diary

- Make a list of all the animals, insects, and birds you have noticed over the last several months.
- List unusual animal and bird sightings and interpretation.
- List recurring sightings.
- List animals or birds reappearing during lifetime.

Exercises

- Write what animal you most resemble, physically and with regard to personality.
- What animal do you think you might have been in a former life?
- Draw the animal that each member of your family seems most like.

Talking To Your Guardian Angel

There are reports from people all over the world who have seen a saint or spirit, depending upon each person's religious framework. Spirits and angels change into the form offering the most comfort and help to those in need. The Great Spirit, the Grandfathers and Grandmothers, the Thunderbeings, the Sun, and other nature or animal deities (interchangeable in their form with humans) were the spirit forms that Native Americans conceptualized as the highest angels. These powerful spirits were more accessible to spiritual leaders, but they listened to prayers made by everyone. The lesser spirits, which were available for everyday help or for practical matters, appeared more often in animal form, but occasionally they came as nature or plant beings.

Everyone today has an angel or spirit guide who will come to his or her aid, if asked. Talking with your guide enables you to ask for solutions to problems and reach better decisions. It is easier than you might imagine to communicate with these heavenly helpers. You may be able to converse the first time you try, but others will need a little practice and

perseverance before communication occurs. Just keep in mind, if you desire it, it will happen. Try the following exercise before reading on.

Always choose a time when you are alone to do your meditation. Burn sage or another smudge and a candle to help attract the angels as well as to clear the room of interfering vibrations. The room should be darkened when you are first learning to concentrate. Eliminate music, ringing phones, and other interruptions.

You should have a strong desire to talk with your guardian angel. If you are totally sincere in your efforts, it will happen. While concentrating, take in three slow deep breaths through your nose and let them out through your mouth. Now energetically clap your hands three times. Close your eyes. Concentrate on looking up toward the center of your forehead with both eyes rolled upward and inward. This is the location of your third eye. Keeping your eyes closed, concentrate on the color that you see before you. The color may or may not be brilliant and it may fade at the edges, so try to define the color as closely as you can. Remember the color.

Repeat the entire exercise in full. If you see the same color, repeat the breathing and the clapping several times, noting any change in color. A Color Visualization Analysis chart can be found in Appendix B on page 215, but it is best NOT to refer to it until you have done this exercise.

Those people having trouble with color visualization need not despair. Anxiety and obsession, which sometimes get in the way, can be overcome by achieving a light trance state before you attempt to talk to your angelic hosts. Use a guided imagery tape, celestial music, relaxation exercise, or self-hypnosis. Precede this with a hot bath or sauna. It will also help if you give up unhealthy foods and alcohol.

After practicing to obtain the highest level color possible (regardless of what color it is), you are ready to begin talking to your spirit guide. Sometimes, intense desire and knowing that you will be able to talk with your guides will catapult you into that vibratory level. Below is a sample

of a conversation designed to bring your guides to you. You do not have to use these exact words; you may use your own. The words of the dialogue are not as important as the sincerity of intentions. However, it is essential that you have your purpose for the discussion clearly in mind before you begin.

◨ DIALOGUE

"Hello, my spiritual friends and advisors, the Grandmothers and the Grandfathers. Thank you for coming to talk with me today. I know I have guardian angels who watch over me. I appreciate your help and want you to know I desire your assistance at all times. I want to become a more spiritual person. I ask you to surround me with white light so that I can attract the highest spirit helpers. I would like to talk with my highest angel available. I ask you now for guidance. I need counsel and advice. The one decision (problem, happening, situation) is _____. What do you advise?"

Begin by letting your own higher self answer your question if you do not "hear or know an answer." Continue to talk and keep the dialogue flowing. When your spirit guides speak, you will know, because the colors behind your closed eyes will begin to change and flutter. The predominant colors should be purples and blues with some silver, gold, or flashes of white light. Do not focus on this process deliberately, because it will disappear as you switch to your left brain analysis. When you find that you are seeing another color, such as yellow, red, orange, or green, you will know that you have taken over the conversation. Relax, take three breaths, intensely desire your guide, clap your hands three times, and begin again. For those persons who are stuck in lower colors, continue your conversation and sincerity of intent and your angels will aid you every way they can, both in your problem and in enabling you to eventually see the purplish hues.

Answers that come from ourselves can occasionally slip in. This usually

occurs when we are thinking of highly emotional issues and of answers that we want to hear. An important decision with suspected ego involvement should be checked out again before acting on the information received. The colors seen will help you decide. Of course, you will know that later when the answers that you received are shown to be incorrect. You are most likely to hear the wrong answers when intense desires intervene or when events affecting your self-esteem or pride are involved.

More often than not, however, you will find yourself amazed with the clarity, depth, and accuracy of the information that you receive. It may be hard to remember all that was said when you emerge from your higher state of being. You will, however, remember the most important solutions and aspects of your questions.

You will eventually develop a "feel" for answers coming from your guides. For example, they will use a different way of talking than you use. They always use the pronoun we. They may refer to you in endearing terms or be humorous. Sometimes you will receive information from them that you do not want to hear. Information may be new to you or unexpected. They present messages in the best way for you to learn from them. The angels are experts in metaphors and N.L.P. (neurolinguistic programming).

They may use a word that you do not know or give you an answer technically beyond your skills or vocabulary. Sometimes, it is necessary to stop the conversation in order to write down words or messages, because when you communicate with your guides, you go into a deep meditative state, bypassing the detailed memory part of the left brain.

Your spirit guides eagerly give help when you use intensity in requesting an answer. Emotion gives power, provided that you do not have an emotional investment in hearing a certain answer. In addition, motivation is important. Your angels will be most eager to help when you are trying to aid other people or work out problems for the good of all.

Your guardian angels wait for your communication. They want to help you improve your life and will accept the challenge eagerly. Your angel spirits have only love for you just as you are. But, they always work for the highest aims and will never hurt anyone else in the process. To help facilitate the communication with your guides, always be as clear and precise as possible with your request or situation. Specifically, what is your question? What do you need to know? Set out to deal with only one question or issue during each meditation.

A VISION QUEST TODAY

It is possible to experience a vision quest today. It is just as valuable an experience as it was in past centuries. The vision quest is one of the oldest sacred journeys sought by humans since they gained a higher consciousness. The hunger for spiritual experiences continues in the present. In some ways, it is easier today, as less strenuous measures are necessary to communicate with our spirit guardians.

Even fifty years ago, sensory deprivation and hardship during a spiritual journey or quest were probably essential to attract your guardian angels, who live in other time and space dimensions. It used to be hard to penetrate through to these outer dimensions for spirit communication. But now, according to those interested in spiritual development, there has been a thinning of the astral veil between earth and the heavens, making it easier to make contact with our angel helpers. We have entered the Age of Aquarius, resulting in world changes and increased astral contact.

Whereas spirit communication has become easier, our earth has become more crowded and noisy, making spiritual pilgrimages more difficult. Common sense rules must be observed when pursuing solitude in an isolated area. The average person does not have the physical strength and stamina that characterized Native Americans in the past.

Imagine your physical condition if you lived outside most of your life, doing physical tasks and eating only natural food and organic game. You drank only pure water and breathed the cleanest air. Imagine never

ingesting any synthetic medicines, chemicals, or additives. None of your food contained sprays or toxins. You walked miles each day on natural terrain.

This was the average way of life for Native Americans. And on top of this, they fasted, used herbs, and did colon cleansing with gourds. Many also took sweat baths in special lodges and bathed in streams and lakes to cleanse their bodies! Many Indians who greeted the white European explorers around the sixteenth century were horrified that these men did not bathe. The Indians knew, instinctively, the truth to the old cliche— cleanliness is next to godliness.

Because most of us do not have the original Native American's constitution, it is necessary to do less strenuous vision quests. There are two main methods. One is to select a "safe place" outside or in a shelter, such as a primitive cabin, in which to be alone. The second is to do a vision quest using imagery. Both methods used together, are even better. Some people like to repeat the quests routinely, at least yearly.

⊟ THE PHYSICAL QUEST

One necessary requirement for your physical vision quest is to be alone. The most difficult part of this quest is finding the right location. Younger, stronger people will want to stay outside in wilderness locations. Other people will want a primitive cabin in a safe, isolated area. For all wilderness quests, it is necessary to have a partner. The partner may be doing a quest, too, but this person must remain totally out of sight. It is usually best to have a meeting place where each person goes at a different time to leave a signal indicating that he or she is all right. A rock left in one spot or a piece of cloth tied to a tree limb each day is the standard signal.

People of differing ages and character types will require different types of locations, and there are many possibilities. Any place, inside or out, with a minimum of comfort and a maximum of safety and isolation, is ideal. You cannot do a vision quest in your own home unless you are an invalid. Our homes surround us with too many distractions and clues that

trigger old practical thoughts and tasks. Find a location that is deserted enough for solitude but suitable for your age and physical condition.

Safe caves make effective locations for the hardy. A cave is guaranteed to make even the most concrete, or left-brained, thinker into a seer of visions. The most potent block to Americans who want to have a vision is the "left-brain syndrome." One must let go of thinking in the ordered, logical, and rational left-brained way in order to let the creative, responsive, right brain take control. Remember, a cave location demands that one take certain safeguards to avoid getting lost or disoriented. Again, a partner is necessary.

The quest is a time of reflection and of delving into one's inner soul. It may provide an opportunity for your guardian angel to send you a message or to reveal itself. This message may be in thought or dream form, or a spirit person or animal may appear to you. All are valid and real. All sensations, feelings, sounds, and images may be important messages from your spirit guides. They chose to appear to you in the form that you desire and are ready to accept you.

The most important purpose of vision quest is spirit communication. Besides the seeking out of your guardian animals or spirits, other vision quests are made to gain insight or to solve problems. You hope to be given some wisdom and knowledge from your guardian spirit.

Vision quests are highly individualistic. It is important that the person state the reason for the quest frequently so that his or her intentions are clear to the spirit helpers. Be specific as to whether you wish the identification of a guardian or solutions to problems from a teacher. It is best that only one agenda be sought at a time.

Fasting should not be attempted during the quest except for those people who have had previous fasting experience. Fasting is one of the oldest methods of increasing spirituality. It is extremely valuable in furthering your spiritual development. However, we must proceed slowly because we have pollution in our bodies that was not present in humans even one hundred years ago. The average American is so full of chemicals

and medicines that even a two-day fast with water could be dangerous. This is because when one stops eating, the chemicals begin to come out of the tissues and to circulate in the bloodstream.

Drinking diluted apple juice as a method of fasting (preceding a vision quest) is recommended. For those who have never fasted and are planning to do a quest, there are certain recommendations. Do not consume meat, salt, processed foods, sugar, soft drinks, desserts, or fatty or rich foods a week before your quest. Your meals should be light and consist mainly of vegetables and whole grains. However, your diet will depend upon your location and facilities. Eat only natural foods and drink pure water and juices. Changing prescription diets, of course, must be discussed with your doctor. Water must always be available for the average American during a quest (to dilute the toxins).

For the first vision quest, it is recommended that a person stay isolated for a period of two to three days. A minimum of noise is crucial. Ideally, you should not see or hear another person for the duration of the quest. You want to exclude all the noises of civilization that you can possibly omit. No phones, newspapers, televisions, radios, or tape recorders should be near. Friends cannot drop by to talk because this will ruin your journey. No activities should be planned, such as hobbies or entertainment. No recreational equipment is recommended except a notebook and pen for jotting down personal revelations. Preparation of food, if there is any, is kept to a bare minimum. Getting less sleep than is normal during the quest helps to facilitate a theta brain wave state.

Other types of vision quest experiences include the use of a float tank, isolation in a darkened room, fire walking, ropes courses, and survival training. More and more vision quest experiences, are being offered by special groups and even by travel agencies. Some of these are excellent opportunities to begin a spiritual awakening. Always trust your own instincts in any new experiences as leaders will have specialties and usually have limited knowledge in some areas.

Some people benefit from staying alone for several days. Being

without company is a thrilling opportunity and a difficult one to accomplish for many people, especially those with large families. Fantastic results can be accomplished by taking a vacation in an outdoor environmental setting. No special rules or deprivation need apply. Simply take a vacation from stress and noise. This is also recommended for people who have difficulty in being alone. Make your first quest a time to be by yourself and to eat and sleep normally.

During your quest, pay special attention to any song or melody that comes to your consciousness. It may be your power song. If it is a familiar melody, analyze the words for hidden clues as to the message that your subconscious is presenting.

Keeping a diary is recommended regardless of the type of quest chosen. Later, these notes can be used to relive your experiences. It is difficult to remember specific events when you are in a strange situation or an altered state of consciousness. The deeper one goes into right-brained thinking, the less chance there is of clear recollection.

Anyone wishing to end his or her quest before the target time can do so without any problem. You just try the next time for a little longer period. A one-day quest is a valuable beginning in obtaining higher consciousness. Start out with a shorter time frame to allow yourself time to conquer your fears. This will enable you to want to extend your stay.

Whatever your quest, know that your effort will be rewarded many times over!

THE UNSEEN WORLD

To see into the fourth dimension of the spiritual world, you should begin two processes. First, do everything you can to develop your higher spiritual self. Many exercises have been given in this book to help you begin your journey. Other printed materials abound at specialty bookstores. Reading about angels is particularly helpful. Seek out experiences that give you a sense of inner wellbeing and satisfaction. Take courses offered by local psychics and spiritual leaders and organizations that will help to develop your senses and your awareness.

Second, and more important, develop an intense desire to view the unseen world. After you have gained the motivation, you will begin to see, feel, and hear into that dimension.

Begin by tuning into your own feelings and intuitions. Trust your instincts and act on the knowledge you have in order to improve your life. You will begin to notice different sensations as you change locations and company. Some places and people will give you a calm, pleasant feeling. Others will cause you to be uncomfortable. Homes will send out the vibrational level of their previous or current owners. Realtors notice that certain homes have cheery personalities but others, possibly with many owners, harbor bad vibrations. Pay attention to people, places, and things that give you a peculiar feeling.

Although you will not want to linger in uncomfortable surroundings, remember your reaction. Your vibrational level will attract or repel the energy around you. Individuals in panic or fear gather undesirable energies to them. You literally can make your fears come true by thinking certain disastrous thoughts. Unfortunately, most of what we think that we see in others is actually a manifestation of our own faults and hidden desires being projected. The one million women (men were rarely suspect!), children, and animals killed during the witch hunts were victims of such paranoia.

If you sense a negative atmosphere, you have only to avoid the places

or people that make you feel uncomfortable. It is important to heed your inner sixth sense as it develops. Undesirable or nonspiritual people can drain your vitality and energy, which limits your higher spiritual development and progress. You can make yourself sick or choose a slow death by living with the wrong person or in an undesirable location.

Bad energies in the atmosphere are usually thought forms (yours are around you more than anyone else's). Remnants of past thoughts or actions, ley lines (magnetic fields), and, occasionally, earthbound entities may have either positive or negative energy. Some ghosts are quite pleasant and are unaware that they are not embodied. Begin to develop your sixth sense so that you will be more aware of the unseen world around you and choose the most desirable company and surroundings.

Spiritual people, churches, sacred ground, power places, and guardian angels emit a sacred essence. You will begin to be sensitive to these vibrational levels and feel their energy and power around you. Seek out and choose these experiences to increase your awareness of the higher planes of existence.

Your first experiences with higher beings may come in the form of seeing faint flickering lights and shadows during meditation or prayer. Seek solitude so that you can be more aware of their presence. Ask for them to come to you and ask for their guidance. You soon will be able to tell when they are near. Some people feel a certain temperature change, when they are around. Others can see slight fluttering movements on the walls or ceilings. Spirits move quickly, and occasionally a change of light or air pattern occurs as a result. It is usually when our eyes are unfocused or looking slightly to the side that we notice these patterns of movement. When we look directly ahead, it anchors our brain to the routine, third dimensional world that we perceive.

Seeing Auras

One of the most common experiences when contacting the fourth dimension is seeing someone who has recently died. What is seen is their etheric or spirit body. This spirit body surrounds the regular, physical body and severs its connection with the physical shell at death. It extends about an inch from the physical person, and is visible only to certain people. However, the ability to see it can be cultivated by you. On of the best ways to begin communication with and awareness of the fourth dimension is to notice the auras surrounding bodies.

Seeing auras requires practice and perseverance. Although individual abilities vary greatly as to skill and to practice time required, most people can learn to see the etheric or physical aura around a person. With much practice, the emotional aura, which surrounds the etheric aura, can be viewed. This is especially true of higher spiritual people, whose auras are quite bright and pronounced. Viewing the mental aura, which extends a foot or two out from the body is harder and usually requires a great deal of practice and effort. The spiritual aura surrounds the mental aura and is the most difficult to see.

The best times to practice are those when you are seated for extended periods, such as during a class, a church service, or a meeting. The classroom, with its green or black chalk-board behind the instructor, is an excellent place to attempt seeing auras. If your teacher's aura has red in it, you'd better complete your assignments!

Churches are even better. Although the minister or priest is not in front of a blackboard, his aura is usually well defined. If you have the opportunity to be around other religious figures such as holy people, medicine men or women, shamans and other healers, you may note an easily visible aura that surrounds their head like a halo. In some cases, you will be able to see an aura going all the way down to a person's feet. If the emotional aura is dark instead of light, you have chosen the wrong teacher.

Ceremonial occasions, such as powwows, weddings, and funerals, are

excellent opportunities to read auras. They often have the added presence of spiritual beings who bring their own essence to the event. Be sure to look for angels as well as the etheric or spirit body of the deceased at funerals. This spirit body is sometimes called the astral body. The deceased will usually attend his or her own funeral, because the astral body remains on the earth plane for four or five days or more before ascending upward to the astral plane. This spirit body of the deceased is often accompanied by angels, who will aid him or her in a future ascent.

Put yourself into a relaxed state by taking deep breaths. As you watch the ceremony, unfocus your eyes slightly to the side of the people involved. At powwows, look between the drummers or dancers for spirit helpers. They will be dressed for the occasion. Look for transparent shadows that move independently of objects around them. During medicine gatherings, look for shadows that have feathers or resemble animals.

At special church services and funerals, look for angels. They appear as luminous shadows with large extensions (these may be wings) on the side, forming the shape of a cross. They are large and are sometimes seen standing next to the wall of the church in front of the congregation. They often stand next to the spirit body of the deceased at a funeral. The deceased's astral body should be standing close to his or her favorite person, invisible to all except those with the sight. The average spirit body will appear as a faint, life-size shadow, which is sometimes easier to see if you are sitting at least twelve feet away. The angels are more luminous and larger.

Auras are composed of some of the same essence that makes up the spirit body. Auras, however, contain colors that reflect the physical, emotional, mental, and spiritual aspects of the living person. The astral, or spirit body, no longer has the physical body with its accompanying chakras, but it does retain the emotional, mental, and spiritual components, which it takes to the astral plane.

Auras are seldom of just one color, although they can be. A spiritual person giving a talk may start out with a yellow aura and end up with a

bluish purple one, as he or she switches from an emotional state to a more mental-spiritual one. Sometimes a holy person or spiritual channeller will have purple, white, or blue colors in his or her halo. Many of the colors in auras change with the type of activities and thoughts. However, people do seem to operate generally out of the same chakras and as a result give off several main colors. You will never see a purple aura on a criminal, for example.

If you want to practice reading auras, do so at work or in a meeting in which you are seated among people and can stare unnoticed at the back of their heads. Or, you and a friend can practice on each other. Use sage to smudge yourselves and the room or burn incense in the room close to your bodies as an alternative. Take deep breaths in through your nose, hold, and breathe out through your mouth until you feel slightly light-headed. Take turns standing up against a white, cream-colored, or very dark wall and examining each other's auras.

The easiest aura to see is the one around the head because it is the brightest and the person's clothes don't obscure the view. As with the rest of the body, the etheric aura is first and extends a little less than an inch from the head. The emotional aura is next, ranging in width from two or three inches to a foot from the body in highly developed folks. The mental body extends out a foot or so from the emotional and the spiritual aura several feet from that. Buddha's spiritual body was supposed to have extended for a mile! So you see there are many variations in size of the spiritual body and few people in our lifetime will be able to see this aura. You can work for years to perfect your skill in reading the easier-to-see etheric or emotional auras.

When you attempt to see a person's aura, do not look directly at him or her. Unfocus your eyes several inches to the right or left of your target area. If you are examining the etheric body, which is close to the body, gaze several inches away from that position. If you are examining the astral or emotional body, you may want to focus some six to eight inches away so that you can pick up the whole span of this aura which averages

around three to four inches from this body. Experiment with training your eyes on different positions of the body.

Try looking at your own aura in an untinted mirror. Look to the side or above your head and stand back from the mirror until you have the best light for viewing. Do not stand beneath a bright light. Sometimes, a side mirror will help you to see the aura from a different perspective, but this is not necessary.

Be persistent and continue to stare off again and again until you pick up the aura. As you turn your eyes to get a better look, you will find that it disappears! This is where patience is required. Do not get discouraged, because eventually you will find that the "sight" becomes easier and requires less time and energy. At first, it may take an hour of practice to get some elusive glimpses that last only several seconds.

Remember that each of the auric layers requires a different focal point because it varies in width from the body. Beginners usually focus on the etheric first, because this is the easiest aura to see.

The etheric or physical body is only an inch or two from a person's body and duplicates its outline like a shadow. A healthy person will have a light, luminous etheric aura. A dark or hard-to-see aura indicates physical problems in the body. The etheric aura may balloon out instead of keeping the form of the body. A dark spot in the aura indicates illness. For example, if the aura around the head is dark, it might indicate mental problems, or depression.

Next, attempt to view the emotional aura. This aura, once detected, will appear in color and is reflective of a person's emotions. While there is some disagreement as to interpretations of shades and hues, most seers generally agree that the purple and white auras are reflective of spiritual persons of high caliber. An indigo aura indicates a person in a higher mental or spiritual state. A blue aura indicates an intellectual. Depending on the clarity and hue, this could be either a controlled, restricted person or a person with a high degree of integration of the mental and spiritual self. Yellow reflects emotion. The pure yellows are

love and devotion, the green-yellows may reflect jealousy and posses-siveness. Interpretation of green in the aura varies with hue and clearness. Muddy green may mean a controlling, stingy person. A clear emerald green will indicate either a strong dedication to a cause or an organized life. A great deal of red in the aura may reflect anger or passion.

Reading a person's emotional and spiritual nature from auric color is for advanced students because many mistakes can be made. The auras change as a person's emotional, mental, and physical states change. The auras will be somewhat different on certain parts of the body, reflecting the condition of each chakra as well as physical and mental problems. The aura is a dynamic, flowing, pulsating aspect of a person. The differ-ent colors will flow together, blend, and separate as influences in parts of the body come together or are overpowered by each other. When you see an aura, you are only observing an aura at one particular time and place, and for this reason you are subject to your own perceptual errors. Sometimes colored clothes reflect into the person's aura and give it a false color. The head aura is usually the easiest to see and subject to fewer errors from the interpreter. In addition, it is the best indicator of the subject's inherent nature.

Do not concern yourself with color at the start. The first step is to see some light or shadow around the body. Always make sure your back-ground or lighting is not giving you shadows in the room. Unfortunately, the backgrounds are not always helpful when it comes to reading an aura. It is best to practice with friends against plain walls. Babies make good subjects because their bodies and minds are still unaffected by environ-ment. A baby may almost glow in the dark. A sleeping baby may be observed at night without his or her objecting.

The Indian Journals 1859–62, *by Lewis Henry Morgan, published by the University of Michigan in 1959, contained the following observations.*

The medicine of the Indian is a misnomer. It means a religious ceremony or an act of worship. Nothing more, nothing less, accompanied when performed for sick persons with such forms as to show the extent of the superstition which penetrates their faith and worship.

The Crows and Minnetares have religious ceremonies regularly at the new and full moon throughout the year. The medicine men are looked to secure favorable weather, the health of the people, good crops, the growth of the grass, the safe birth of children....

At the new moon there is a general meeting of the medicine men called by those who...collect for a feast on this occasion. As soon as they come together they commence singing. They make a bed of coals, and then burn pine leaves, or any herb which they may have or sweet grass and thus raise a species of incense. They hold each of them their medicine bag in the smoke.

Chapter Seven

MEDICINE

The word *medicine* in the Native American sense means a movement of energy with effects not explained except by the supernatural or mysterious. Medicine is invisible and intangible, the Indians' conception of the one force animating all life.

Power, or medicine, results from receiving favor and strength from the Great Spirit, whose energy extends to plants, animals, and nature beings. These spirit helpers let the Indians "borrow" attributes in time of need and granted wishes—like the Christian angelic forces that perform miracles to help people on Earth. Surveys show 80 percent of Americans believe in the existence of angels.

To Native Americans, health, food, and survival depended on higher powers, such as the animal and plant beings, to provide crops, survival skills and, sometimes, life itself. Through prayer, ritual, reference and ceremony to the Being, or Beings, Native Americans asked to become one with the spirit, to acquire the spirit's characteristics for themselves. This gave them power. If you had "medicine," you had power.

Healing with herbs was only one way cures were achieved. Generally healing granted by spirits ranked above physical cures, although physical cures helped. Today we know the spiritual/mental/emotional dimension is as important to healing as are physical medicines.

POWER RITUALS

The most powerful rituals are those accompanied by joy and celebration. Two ingredients must be present: emotion and action. The action may be physical or it may be mental. Native Americans, as mentioned, depended to a great extent on song and prayer for their power. It was believed that a song was given to them by the spirits, and it was what enabled them to have power. If you are serious about walking the Rainbow Path, then you will need to find your power song. You also will need prayers, which should be simple and uniquely yours. Those with the highest requests receive the fastest attention.

The amount of ritual performed by Native Americans would surprise most people. Some ceremonies last for many days, during which memorized behaviors, songs, and prayers were enacted. A Piegan (Blackfoot) Indian Beaver Bundle ceremony was reported to have had more than three hundred songs or repetitions that had to be sung!

The importance of ritual in obtaining power is overlooked in our society. Ritual quiets the mind, making it accessible for spiritual acts, and a quiet mind blocks out negativity and wasted energy. Spiritual songs and prayers give power to the person performing them. The power of thought control used in a ritualistic act was known and practiced by the Native Americans.

For example, the words, "power, powerful, it is powerful, I am powerful, they are powerful, her medicine is powerful, the smudge is powerful," are used in Native American ceremonies. By repeating the words, their energy is released. Remember, Native Americans used such words to ask for attention and blessings from their spiritual helpers. To be granted the power, you must request it from your supernatural helpers and ask that it be used for the betterment of all. To use your power for anything but the highest aims will result in problems for yourself. The stronger the power granted, the more repercussions you will suffer if it is misused. Beware!

EMPOWERING YOURSELF AND OBJECTS

To increase the intensity of your energy and to empower objects with vibrations, use the following rituals:

- Smudge yourself and place an object so that it faces one of the four directions.
- Turn and face each of the four directions, both standing and bowing.
- Shake your rattle above your head and below your waist in each direction.
- Blow tobacco smoke (or offer tobacco) above your head and below your waist to each direction.
- Say a prayer to each direction, above and below.
- Sing your song to each direction, above and below.
- Dance your power animal in each direction, above and below.
- Burn smudge toward each direction, above and below.
- Offer cornmeal to each direction, above and below.

Now face the object toward the next direction and repeat each of the above steps. Repeat until the object has been blessed in each direction. Each time the object is moved, repeat the words, "I am powerful, this (name the object) is powerful. My medicine is powerful, the (name the object) is powerful."

Suggested articles to empower are personal objects, totems, feathers, crystals, stones, and jewelry.

◧ POWER SONG

You can find your power song by yourself or with the help of a drumming group. Burn sage or incense and listen to a drumming tape or beat a drum yourself. Then, with your eyes closed, allow yourself to totally relax and concentrate on the beat. You will eventually hear words or music that will form a rhythm. Let yourself go and experiment with the words or tune. Sing it over and over until you remember the sequence. Sing whatever comes to mind. All you need are several phrases with a melody. If doing this in a group, anyone receiving a phrase or song should sing aloud spontaneously, then wait for another to find his or her song. The song that comes to you may be your power song.

Do not let others know your song except during a medicine gathering. Remember the song and write it down. When you need to use your medicine, sing your song. If you cannot sing aloud, sing to yourself. Use this song whenever possible. It will gain in power as it is used.

Medicine Bags

Each medicine man or woman possessed a medicine bag made from animal skin that contained power objects for healing. The contents of each bag varied in size and number, but most contained bird or animal bones, tails, feathers, or claws and an assortment of herbs or roots, smudges, paints, rocks, or other symbolic articles to represent a deity, such as the sun. Of supreme importance, even more than the contents of the bag, was the song each shaman possessed. The song was sung while the medicine objects were being used during ceremonies. The song, given by the spirits, was the catalyst for releasing powers.

Today, we have only the animal and bird body parts, which are more or less dropped on our doorstep. The contemporary medicine person does not need to kill for food and would never capture an animal or bird for his or her medicine. If you are truly walking the Rainbow Path, opportunities to gather personal power objects, feathers, and even dead birds, will appear. Dead birds and wild animals appear in a synchronistic fashion to a person, much as the live ones do.

◧ Road Kills

One source for feathers or skins are "road kills." To be prepared for road kills, always travel with plastic bags, a sack of salt, a sharp knife, gloves, sage, a small shovel or trowel, and a paper bag for burial.

When you see a dead creature by the road, pull over safely off the road and examine it. The first items found for your bag may be the most important ones and will be lifetime power articles. If it is a bird with wings both folded in toward the body (instead of at least one wing sticking out away from the body), if it is badly decomposed, or if it is a skunk (rabies carrier), leave it alone. If the specimen is not decomposed, and you have a feeling it was meant for you to find, you have two options.

First, you can put on your gloves, place the animal or bird in your plastic bag, cover it with salt, and take it home. If it is a dead owl, eagle, or other protected species, decide whether you want it in your car. You cannot prove it was hit by a car before you found it.

Second, if you wish only the feathers from your specimen, use your knife to cut away the two wing sections and one tail section, put them in your plastic bag, cover them with salt, and put them in your car trunk. When you get home, select a cardboard box large enough to spread the feathers attached to the wing. Cover the bottom of the box with a layer of salt (you will need a large amount, and pickling or regular salt, which is sold in bulk, are good choices to use). Spread out the wings in the cardboard box. Place a thick layer of salt over the entire wing, including the feathers. The salt will preserve the wing by drawing the moisture out of the meat. Leave the wing in the salt for at least six weeks. Do not cover the cardboard box. Leave the wing in the salt until there is no odor. Remember, once dried in place, you cannot rearrange the feather spread, so they must be placed as you want them.

Small animal skins (separated from the body) may be temporarily covered with salt, until the proper curing procedure is performed. Kits may be purchased if you wish to do it yourself. Small animals can be taken to a professional curer. Large animals should be left where they are found after a blessing of sage and a prayer to hasten their journey toward the Rainbow Path. Always use gloves when handling dead animals or birds.

Small animals or birds can be buried in a paper sack, using your

shovel. Sprinkle sage before covering them and ask that their journey be a good one. Leave undesirable animals (decomposed, etc.) where you found them, untouched, with a sprinkling of sage, if desired.

⊞ CONTEMPORARY MEDICINE BAGS

Because we may not have many wild animal skins and parts for our medicine bag, we add more stones, crystals, and amulets to them instead. Feathers are important, and as mentioned, you will have many opportunities to find them.

Most medicine bags today are used by an owner to increase his or her own spirituality and sacred power. Medicine used for manipulation of others will inevitably come back on the user. It is permissible to increase your own power *for the good of all*. If you have an important meeting where you wish to present yourself in the best possible way, take your medicine bag with you in your briefcase or pocket where it cannot be seen. If you are in a conflict situation with another person, use your medicine bag for power but always make it clear that the outcome you desire from your power is *for the good of all involved*. In other words, use your power to better yourself, not to defeat another. Always check your motives and ask that others be considered.

On the Rainbow Path, many objects will come your way that will interest you or seem significant. After discovering your power animal, you may find small carvings or statues of this particular creature and others may give you feathers or stones. Put these in your medicine bag. They may be important power articles. Eventually, you will have collected so many items that it will be necessary to choose only the most significant—the space in your bag will be limited.

Helpful items such as cornmeal, sage, and herbs are often placed in a secondary bag. In addition, larger items, such as rattles and large feathers, can be wrapped in larger bundles. Drums and blankets are handled singularly because of their bulk.

Sample Medicine Bag Contents
Feathers from power birds or birds
Animal skin, whole or partial
Crystals (type depends upon need)
Stones (type depends upon use)
Fetish (purchased from a Native American—usually a carving—may depict a power animal)
Jewelry (if it contains a special stone or is symbolic)
Amulet (these are symbolic, may be a cross or other religious object)
Special insect or butterfly (in tiny bag)
Any item with special significance

Occasionally, a piece of jewelry may be taken out of the bag and worn. However, except for stones, which are changed as particular needs are desired, the rest of your bag should remain intact and in a safe place. It should be small enough to be placed in a large pocket but ample enough to hold your supplies. The best bags are made from soft animal skins fashioned by Native Americans. Do not buy objects decorated with animal skins unless you feel drawn to those particular items, because it promotes trapping and killing. You will have ample opportunity to obtain animal articles.

Each item in your medicine bag is representative of sacred power. Each item is essentially a talisman. It reflects the power of its owner, a person, an animal, or a community, just as the American flag reflects the essence of America.

HEALING CRYSTALS

Crystals have been used by healers and diviners since humans originated. Each type of crystal has unique qualities and healing specialties. Virgin crystals handpicked from the mines are the best because they have had no previous owners and therefore no old programming. If you do not live in Arkansas or a state with crystal mines, then you can purchase one.

When you buy a crystal, it will have been handled by other people and will need to be cleansed of vibrations. Take your crystal and place it in salt water, made by adding a pinch of salt (sea salt is best) in a small glass of tepid water. Leave it there for a week for the initial cleansing and for several hours, or until it achieves its former clearness after every healing session.

Other ways to cleanse crystals, which are less convenient perhaps, are to immerse them in a running stream or ocean, bury them in Mother Earth, or smudge them well on all sides with sweet-smelling (high quality) sage. Those crystals not used for healing can be placed in direct sunlight to be recharged.

If you wear your crystal, you will notice that it clouds up after it has absorbed energies. Leave it in a salt-water solution until it becomes clear again. This will enable the crystal to continue healing with its energies at full strength. Crystals heal by sending out magnetic energy fields at desirable vibrational levels. Problem areas in the body have distorted or undesirable vibrational levels, and crystals help remove positive (undesirable) ions from the energy fields and substitute negative (desirable) ions.

Some experts believe that crystals amplify the energy around them if the energy resonates with the crystal. Remember that you have an energy field determined by your thoughts. Increase your power by using a crystal to help you broadcast your desires. Practice sending self-improvement messages while holding or wearing your crystal. The crystal also deflects

undesirable vibrations and can break from the impact. The crystal can heal by sending out desirable vibrations and deflecting unwanted energies.

The crystals used most frequently for healing are clear quartz crystals. Usually the size should be at least four inches long with a well defined point. Do not buy a crystal with a broken point or end, because this is its antenna. You hold the crystal in your right hand with the point outward unless you are working on yourself. You always go in a counterclockwise direction when healing.

To program your crystal, hold it in your hand and give it a message or directive. You do not need to say it aloud. Just think it. For example, *please remove all positive ions from this person's chakras.* Or say, "I wish to feel joy today. I am going to fill you with the joy vibration and then wear you so that you will help me retain this energy." After doing this, feel joy going all through your body as you hold your crystal in your *right* hand, pointing it toward yourself.

You receive energy from your left side and give it out from your right side. Therefore, you always heal with the right hand. The left side is the feminine or receptive side and the right side of the body is the masculine or giving side. This is true in people who are left-handed as well as right-handed. Crystals can be used on chakras and problem areas or worn for increased well-being.

When healing others while holding a pointed crystal, always anchor yourself by imagining the healing energy coming from above you, through you and into the crystal and person. You do not provide the healing yourself, you channel the divine energy from above. This procedure does not deplete you and protects you from absorbing anyone else's vibrations. After healing and placing the crystal in salt water, flick your hands down to the ground, then rinse both hands in cool water. Feel all the unwanted energy leaving your hands and flowing into the water.

When wearing a crystal, select one that helps you accomplish your own healing. If you wear a small crystal with a point, the point should

hang down toward your body. If you wear crystal jewelry, pick out a type of crystal that will harmonize with needed healing work.

Crystals that have been subjected to high heat in order to change their colors cannot be used to heal. Many stones are routinely radiated to change their colors. Some of these are amethyst, aquamarine, citrine, sapphire, topaz, colored diamonds, turquoise, and emeralds. If the color seems unusually bright, always ask if the stone has been heat-treated. It is not necessary to have bright colors. A pale stone, such as a light amethyst, works beautifully.

When worn around the neck, amethyst helps the throat chakra and brings spiritual thoughts to the mind. Worn over the heart, it protects and heals. This is especially helpful for people who work in high stress situations or for those in the health fields subject to the burnout syndrome.

An amethyst crystal used on the head chakras is powerful enough to give you a headache if used too long. Do not sleep with a large amethyst crystal by your bed because it will keep you awake! This is also true for citrine crystal, which is yellow, or smoky quartz. The amethyst, citrine, and smoky quartz crystals are safely used in jewelry. They retain some power when cut into shapes. The large ones in crystal form are marvelous for increasing spiritual vibrations in your room and for promoting change and insights. They are known for their ability to help a person with a breakthrough, whether physical, emotional, mental, or spiritual. For lazy glands, use a citrine, amethyst, or smoky quartz crystal with a point to jolt them into action. To avoid tears in the aura, use sparingly.

Clear crystals with natural points are the ones used for clearing chakras and for general work on the body. Use the same crystal for the same task. Do not use one for healing one day and to increase vitality in the room the next day. Only use certain crystals for healing. Do not let other people use your crystals and do not wear or borrow another's stones. Crystals that are always used for the same purpose increase in programming and power. If you mix up their uses, you will scramble their computer.

For medicine, use your crystals for three main purposes:

1. Healing others or working on specific locations. Use a clear crystal with a point.
2. Wearing as jewelry with a specific goal for healing in mind.
3. Using as senders and receivers in a room or medicine wheel. For these, use the large crystals or rocks in natural form. Some of these have a beauty that is indescribable.

◧ USES OF HEALING CRYSTALS

Quartz crystals (the best conductors and healers) are classified into two main categories: The glassy crystals and the dense or opaque crystals. Stones and crystals also can be a mixture of the two types. Amethyst can be either clear like a diamond or opaque. Cat's eye, jasper, onyx, and carnelian are types of crystals that are often opaque. Some healers believe the clear, glassy, quartz crystal to be the best conductor and healer. However, all stones have useful properties and thus you have a whole drugstore of mineral helpers waiting for you to use them. Incidentally, minerals and stones love to have human contact.

◧ MINERALS TO USE IN YOUR MEDICINE BAG:

Amethyst

One of the most popular stones, it can be expensive or inexpensive, clear or opaque, and can be fashioned into any type of jewelry. It is also found in crystals with points that are a foot long! How would you like to have that mineral friend as a helper? They are also found growing in round stones that are cut open to reveal the crystal growth (geodes) inside. Some of these, as well as the larger crystal stones, cost thousands of dollars. A polished, opaque amethyst may cost fifty cents. Use your amethyst for increasing your spiritual vibrations and for becoming more psychic. If you are one of the rare spiritual types who need "grounding," avoid this stone unless you are a healer. If so, wear a small amethyst over your heart for protection against burnout.

Black Tourmaline

This beautiful stone is usually not found in bulk, and a small, unset stone may cost around ten dollars. This stone is unexcelled for providing protection against environmental stresses. It gives you more endurance in crisis situations. It makes attractive jewelry and can be worn as earrings or necklaces. To give you the most protection, wear a loose stone in your left pocket. This will block negative influences such as anger or fear from entering your aura. Black onyx is also effective the same uses and is frequently made into jewelry. For less expensive alternatives, use black apache tears or black or snowflake obsidian. These stones are readily available and provide excellent protection in traumatic situations. Include them in your medicine bag, which is hung on the left side of your body to provide a shield for your aura.

Citrine

A yellow- or gold-colored crystal that is often glassy in appearance and resembles a yellow topaz or diamond. It is not as well known but is one of the most useful minerals. Like the amethyst, it can be found in large opaque pieces as well as in tiny diamond-like gems. It is also found in crystal form with a point. Do not use the pointed crystal for healing as it is too powerful. Place it several feet from your bedstand so that it will not keep you awake, and it will help increase your psychic abilities and promote needed change in your life. This is the stone for students who need to increase their study skills and mental clarity. Wear it in shaped, jewelry form around your neck to increase your verbal abilities or wear or tape it on your solar plexus chakra to promote emotional growth—it helps to work through fear and anger.

Green Adventurine

Use this stone with another variety of quartz crystal, tiger's eye, to increase your luck in money matters. Always carry one or both of these stones in your purse, money pocket, or wallet, as close to the money as

possible. Whenever you see it, think prosperity and this will program it into increased action. Use a larger stone of green adventurine or tiger's eye to set on your desk at your business location or any place where luck and good fortune are needed. These stones give you a good feeling just to look at them!

Other powerful, green healing stones that are excellent for the physical body are turquoise, emerald, green tourmaline, and peridot.

Red Jasper

This is an inexpensive stone that is an excellent grounding mineral. Carnelian is another red stone that provides grounding and is often used in jewelry. These stones are for those people who need to avoid amethyst. It will bring you right down to earth and help keep you focused. It is a must for disorganized people or those who procrastinate. All red stones are to be avoided by those people with serious physical illnesses or with manic personalities, as it can exacerbate these problems. Substitute hematite, flint, or petrified wood as inexpensive, nonstimulating alternatives. Healthy but tired or depressed people are those most likely to benefit from red stones.

Rose Quartz

This quartz is pink or rose colored. It is an inexpensive helper stone. This stone is often found in a mass, such as a boulder. A large, pink quartz for your medicine wheel or yard will cost only a few dollars. This stone is often shaped into beads, which are used to make necklaces. The rose quartz necklaces that come down to your heart center are unexcelled for healing the heart chakra. Wear this stone when recovering from the loss of a loved one. Others who fear intimacy can wear this stone to open their heart chakra. Men or women who need this stone and do not want to wear beads, can wear a rose-quartz crystal with the point down. Have it set with some onyx on the side if you wish some protection while risking new relationships.

Beside the uses that I have mentioned, small stones can be taped to the body on specific locations, such as chakra spots or areas of physical ailments. Use more than one for greater effect. For example, tape a blue azurite or amethyst to your forehead to increase your dreams or tape a citrine, amethyst, lapis lazuli, or sodalite on your throat chakra to increase psychic hearing and verbal abilities. Tape a small rose quartz to your heart at night for healing and any of the green healing stones mentioned above to your solar plexus to give you more self-confidence and to overcome fear and anger. Use a small carnelian, bloodstone, ruby, or red garnet to revive lost sexual energy.

All of these stones are to be worn periodically, as needed, and cleansed after prolonged use. The ultimate goal for a medicine man or woman is balance; balance in the chakras, and in the physical, emotional, mental, and spiritual bodies. Without this, energy cannot flow up and down your body and cannot be used to heal others. In addition, you cannot receive higher communications from spirit helpers if your chakras are not open to receive the vibrations. Blocked chakras will stop the flow of the vital, sacred energy that you will need for your spiritual journeys.

POWER BUNDLES

A medicine bag remains with a person throughout his or her lifetime. Even today, many Native American tribes have community power bundles carefully guarded by select persons. These bundles are opened only at special times and the contents are considered sacred and untouchable.

Today, individuals can make their own power bundles in two different ways. The first is to compile a large bundle using one's totems and sacred objects. This type is usually prepared during crisis situations or in times of need.

The second type of power bundle is small and is buried in Mother Earth or hung on a tree or bush. You do not see this offering again. You present this bundle as a request for certain favors and for powers to be received. For increased energy, bundles are presented or buried during certain celestial times, such as the new moon, the full moon, the shortest day of the year, the longest day of the year, the day of the first thunderclap in the spring, the day of the summer or winter solstice, of the fall or spring equinox, or of a solar or lunar eclipse.

If you wish for quick results, prepare your power bundle during the full moon. If you want help developing a new project, bury your power bundle at the height of the new moon. If you wish to ease your pain because of an ending relationship, choose a lunar eclipse or waning moon. The spring equinox is a good time for planting seeds and for beginning new lives and projects. The fall and winter help transformation and the severing of old ways and attachments.

The bundles in your possession are kept until either your wish is granted or the situation in question is resolved. These bundles contain articles similar to the smaller offering bundles except there is no limit to the number of articles that you can use. They are disassembled when desired, but the contents are retained.

Power Bundle Materials

Natural cloth (choose from five colors: black, white, red, blue, and yellow)

Red twine or string

Cornmeal and tobacco

Sage, juniper, and cedar (You can substitute a local smudge for one of these, such as sweetgrass, red willow, carrot root, piñon, or mesquite.)

Lock of your hair

Strip of paper with your wish on it

Symbol representing your wish (picture, article, name)

Small rock or stone

Small totem to give away (for offering bundle)

Totems, stones, crystals, jewelry, photographs (for larger bundle)

Power Bundle Directions

Cut your cloth into six-inch or eight-inch squares for offering bundles and any size desired for the larger bundle. Different tribes used different colors to represent the four directions but they almost always chose from one of the five colors mentioned previously. Skins, leather, or suede can be used in place of the cloth for the larger one.

Tie each small bundle with red yarn after its contents are added. Use only a pinch of your herbs or offerings and choose small items. Tie your larger bundle with either a leather strip or red yarn.

Write your wish on a strip of paper and enclose it. Your wish must be specific as to the action desired. If the wish is "feminine" (creativity, love, receiving), add cornmeal. If the wish needs "masculine" energy (logic, aggression, analytical thought), use tobacco. Use both, if you want both energies. For the other plant offerings—sage, juniper, and cedar—it is permissible to substitute one plant that is native to your area.

A lock of your hair is always enclosed. For an offering bundle, add a gift of a tiny mineral or pebble and totem that you like, such as a small feather, a crystal, a flower, or a souvenir. Add a symbol if you have one.

For example, a health wish might include a picture of yourself in good health or a wish for a raise might include play money or a sketch of your boss handing you a check. Love wishes might include a valentine or poem. Fold these up so that they are small enough to fit into the bundle.

After your smaller offering is complete, bury it or hang on a bush or tree on the day you have chosen. Sunrise, sunset and the new or full moons are powerful times to offer your bundle.

A larger bundle, which you will keep, can include appropriate tarot cards. Add any additional objects to this power bundle, fold up, tie, and store in a place where it will be undisturbed.

Eileen Nauman, who has Cherokee ancestry, refers to the offered power bundles as prayer bundles. She presents her bundles to Mother Earth for burial or hangs them on a bush or tree. She says that your first four bundles are the most important. She suggests using four different colors to represent the four directions and using the color appropriate for the wish.

She uses black for north, yellow for east, red for south, and blue for west. Put the request for business direction or power in a black cloth. A wish requesting change or transformation goes in a blue cloth. A yellow cloth, representing the east, is appropriate for a request for ideas, for creativity or for beginning projects. Requests for money or love go in the red cloth of the south.

Make your first four prayer bundles for yourself. Do one for each direction. After two weeks, you can make bundles for other people at their request. Nauman smudges before she does a prayer bundle. She always asks Mother Earth for permission to bury the bundle. She digs a hole, puts in an offering of sage, tobacco, juniper or cedar, buries the bundle, and then adds more of the aforementioned offering before covering up the bundle. She adds a feather to any bundle tied to a tree or bush. The different bundles can be offered on the same night or spaced out.

Do not dig up your bundle or go out to check its condition. It will disappear when the wish is granted. You must be careful what you wish, because if it is right for you, you will get what you asked. Wishes cannot

be retracted. Some wishes will be granted in several days, others will take several months. Give extra power to your bundle by directing positive thoughts and emotions toward obtaining your goals.

FEELING DIAGNOSIS

Before beginning to diagnose or heal illness, always cleanse the room and the people in it with the smoke of sage or cedar. The dried leaves may be bound together in a smudge stick or crushed into a pile that is dense enough to smolder. Both sage and cedar grow wild in most areas and are easily obtained. Never over-pick your source and never pick during times of drought. Always ask permission from Mother Earth to pick the leaves and always leave the root intact.

The best way to obtain sage or cedar is to purchase it from businesses marketing smudge sticks that take environmental concerns into account. When possible, check their sources and find out how they replenish their supplies or if they grow them. You also can buy sage from nurseries or grow your own in an herb garden. Cedar is more plentiful in the wild and is easily grown in your yard. Be careful to ask permission and not damage the trees.

Once you obtain your sage or cedar, light it and then blow out the flame so that it smolders and throws off smoke. Put it in a container that is bigger than the smudge so that there is no danger of fire. Light it in a place where any loose spark won't ignite the surroundings. Only use very small amounts so that the sparks and smoke are contained. Using a feather fan or other spreading device, make sure that the smoke permeates whatever you are cleansing. It is best to start with the room. Then, fan the smudge onto both the front and back of the person who is to be worked on. Smoke yourself by setting the smoldering sage down and turning your front and back toward it to cleanse yourself. You can use a fan to help cover yourself.

Draperies or upholstery will absorb the resins from the smoke; so do

not overdo your cleansing. It is not necessary to fill the room with smoke or to make anyone cough or be uncomfortable. A little smoke is powerful and goes a long way toward cleansing both room and people of undesirable vibrations.

The feeling analysis for trouble spots in the body is done with the hands. You will not touch the person, only his or her aura, which will be out several inches to a foot or more from the body. By moving your hand gently toward the person, thereby compressing the space between your hand and the person's body, you will be able to feel different sensations. Unless you can see auras, you will be analyzing solely from touch. Remove all jewelry and only wear clothing made of natural fibers when doing your analysis. Ask your client to put any jewelry in a purse or billfold.

You will check for hot spots, cold spots, dead spots, power spots, vibrating spots, and sensations in your own hands, such as tingling or numbness. The different sensory feedback and its meaning will be subjective. As you begin to use your hand, you will form your own data for interpretation. It will be necessary to practice before you analyze with skill. However, many people can locate troublesome areas in the body the first time they try.

Cold spots mean a blocked or congested area. The colder the area, the more blockage there is. It is interesting that the name for the common cold also describes the sensation that it produces in the hands. Feel the aura over the face of a person who has a cold and you will feel the chill. Cold spots may indicate chronic problems where circulation is impaired or blockages are present. These closed areas can be improved with healing energy. As you might suspect, the physical and emotional auras can be affected with problems in any area.

Hot areas are more serious and indicate long term tissue damage or auric shutdown. They may indicate diseased or "burned out" areas. These are usually characteriological, meaning characteristic of a person with a particular personality and physical constitution. A hot aura around the

head may indicate a person who focuses on the negative or has a chemical imbalance or pituitary weakness. A hot spot in the pelvic area may mean disease or an obsession with sex.

Flat or dead spots represent a lack of vitality or emotion, usually due to repression. Physically, they may signify organ removal or surgery. Flat spots in the pelvic area may mean the person has had sexual organs removed or has no sex life.

Diffuse scattered vibrations often indicate that a person has conflicting intentions or is confused. These areas may indicate an inherent weakness in the body or a tendency to be nonfocused or indecisive. There may also be static electricity, which interferes with receiving positive electrons and brings discord.

If one hand tingles or feels numb, check out the same spot with the other hand. This is usually indicative of static electricity or of problems in the body. If so, more analysis is needed to determine the reason.

Occasionally, you will encounter a person whose aura is so powerful that you feel the pressure of it pushing against your hands as you attempt to compress inward. This may mean a healer or person of tremendous spiritual energy, or it may mean a person who is extremely emotional and is propelling all his or her vitality outward.

In order to make a differential diagnosis, you need the person's permission and cooperation. As will be discussed later, questions and inquiries are helpful. Intrusive questions are unnecessary, because the person will usually volunteer the information that you need. Never show any emotion if something feels bad or serious. Because all work is experimental and your ethics do not permit scaring someone, quietly comment and ask for further information. No matter how skilled you become, it is not your place to offer differential diagnosis. Your analysis also could be incorrect. Assessment is done to locate areas that are in need of healing and to offer general feedback to the person so if he desires, he can continue improving himself.

Before you begin your analysis, take a deep breath through your nose

and breathe out through your mouth. Repeat this breathing several times and, while you are doing this, picture vines rooted deeply in the earth entwining your ankles to anchor and center you. Picture the sun coming from the other direction (above you) and encapsulating you in a golden cocoon of healing energy. Imagine this vital solar energy coming down into you through the top of your head.

The above exercise will help to keep your resources from being depleted and will give you more available healing energy. It will also ground you. Vibrations received from above insure healing energies from high sources so that you don't have to use your own and grounding ensures that all undesirable energies will not stay in your body. This is particularly important for "givers," who frequently expend too much of their own energy and end up depleted. Working on the auras of others without these steps can be dangerous.

If, after following these steps, you find yourself exhausted or weak, you need to delay your healing career until you have strengthened your own aura and removed negative influences from around you. If you continue working with other people's auras, you could deplete your energy supply to such dangerous levels that you would not have the resources to throw off negative material and literally could catch another person's problem.

After doing your breathing and grounding exercises, you are ready to begin your feeling diagnosis. Explain to the person that you want him or her to practice breathing in and out calmly while you feel the vibrations around his or her body. Tell the person that he or she can either leave his or her eyes open or close them and that you will begin at the back and move to the front.

As you move your hands, you will be no closer than several inches from the person's body. You may want to come out eight or nine inches or more at certain times. Begin by doing an overall assessment with both palms simultaneously, making sure that your fingertips are pointing up and you are facing the back of the person. Move your hands together in

unison and sweep across the back area beginning at the head and coming down. When you get lower, you will want to reverse your palms so that the fingertips are down. Do this slowly enough to measure any sensations. Then switch to the front and work your way down. I usually start by having the person sit down and then ask the person to stand when doing the back side. If the person is tall, ask him or her to sit while you do the head and shoulder area from behind.

This preliminary assessment will give you a general idea as to a person's energies. Let your mind be as clear as possible and note any thoughts that enter your mind at the same time you are feeling with your hands. Remember, do not touch the body—you should be out at least several inches from it.

The next movement focuses on specific sensations and is done with one hand on one side of the body and the other hand on the other side of the body. You will be facing the side of the person. You will examine the whole body as well as the chakras. This technique is valuable because you can check out a sensation felt with one hand by switching to the other. Sometimes I ask the person to turn slightly if I am checking out drafts in the room. If you experience the same sensation with the other hand, then you have verified your data.

Begin this analysis by coming down from the top several feet above the person's head and working closer to the crown. Check the crown chakra without pushing too hard on that area. Proceed slowly, stopping when you feel compression against your hands. If you press down too hard and too close it could be uncomfortable for the person. If you feel resistant pressure at eight or nine inches, stop there.

After doing the crown chakra, come down, still keeping one hand on each side, and measure the third-eye chakra. One hand is level and perpendicular in front between the eyes and the other hand is behind the head at the same horizontal level. While in this area, check the head, switching sides with your hands before moving on. Mentally note what

you find. Do not comment on any findings until you have completed your analysis.

After moving down from the head, survey the shoulders and the top of the chest. The throat chakra is checked separately. Again, avoid pushing too forcefully against it. If you feel significant sensations, rotate both hands (attempt to duplicate sensation with the other hand) and ask the person to move slightly. This helps guard against any sensations that might be coming from your own hand or from any draft in the room.

The heart chakra is assessed next with the lower half of the chest. One hand will be in front of the heart and the other will feel the back at the same level. At this point, ask your client to stand for the examination of the lower half of the body.

The solar plexus chakra is right above the navel. Check this area along with the abdomen. The root chakra is at the base of the spine. Again, test both front and back locations at the same time. Sensations are double-checked by switching hands. After completing the torso, finish by going down both legs to the feet.

Now you have completed your examination. Depending on the client, you may ask a few questions as you proceed. Notes are helpful if numerous problem areas are located. Otherwise, delay all comments and questions until completion of the diagnosis.

After surveying the whole body, go back and discuss any difficulties that your client has experienced in relation to the particular areas that you have flagged. Say as little as possible about your finding and use words like "cold spot" or "hot spot." It will not help anything if you tell your fears or dramatic findings.

A person cannot tell you the condition of his or her chakras and you may or may not want to share what you have discovered. If, however, you are going to do any healing on that chakra, then it is imperative that you ask the person's permission and share your findings so that he or she can give consent to your healing work. This will keep you out of the realm or working in secret and will include the client in the healing and awareness process, making your healing more effective.

You will discover a relationship between the physical (etheric) and emotional (astral) auras. Difficulty in one area always results in repercussions or accompanying problems in the other.

A closed or blocked third-eye chakra may mean panic states or someone with tunnel vision. Such a person may have had chemical imbalances or suffer from depression or manifest denial.

A cold throat chakra tells you that the person does not say what he or she thinks. A cold heart chakra may reveal a person who has closed off emotions for protection. A hot area may mean disease or malfunction in the organ or glands. Heart and heart chakra problems are often related to inabilities to give and receive love, problems usually developed during childhood.

Solar plexus sensations indicate control issues or holding in of negative emotions. This includes fear and anger. Resultant effects are reflected in the liver, kidneys, small intestines, and stomach.

The lower chakra demonstrates problems in the sex organs, urinary tract, and appendix. This area is important to a person's stability and security.

Other locations on the body such as the thigh or knee, will reflect difficulties in that area.

The healer never pretends to be a physician or other kind of healer. He or she is simply doing a spiritual analysis that may or may not yield information to be of assistance to someone. Never make claims or say that you will treat any disease. It is better if no specific disease is mentioned by you. Never agree to treat a certain problem or suggest that the person stop seeing his physician.

After all, your treatment is an energy procedure and has nothing to do with a particular problem or with treating certain disorders. Any healing or assistance you do is only through light and energy channelled down from high sources. Therefore, any healing done is not enacted by you personally.

After analysis, begin healing. It is not necessary to know a reason for the problem or even have an idea why areas demonstrate certain sensations. You merely identify these areas so you will know where to concentrate your healing energies. Any insight about the difficulty is for the client to use for increased awareness.

Before you begin again, repeat your exercise of deep breathing—in through your nose and out through your mouth. Imagine vines rooted deeply in the earth entwining your ankles to anchor and center you. Picture the sun coming from above your head and encapsulating you in a golden cocoon of healing energy. Feel this vital solar energy coming down into you through the top of your head and going out your feet into the ground. By having the light come down into and through your body, you protect your vitality and keep yourself from absorbing unwanted energies from your clients.

Envision this healing light coming through your hands. Place your hands several inches from the person's body in the areas that most need healing. Then go over the spot repeatedly with a downward stroking motion, keeping your hands out from the body several inches. Let the light from your hands soothe and heal this area. Feel the energy penetrating the person's body, bringing energy and health. If desired, hold your hand in a fixed position for a while before resuming your "petting" or downward stroking.

Move to the next area that must be energized. Repeat the healing process. After energizing the area, move to any others that you have found. After working on specific locations, finish your healing process by lightly stroking the whole body again in a downward motion. Remember, you are not touching the body, only the aura. This seals and closes the auras and gives the person a feeling of well-being.

After healing, always flick off your hands the energy that you have received and wash them with cool running water. Energy treatments may have to be repeated for best results, but wait several days or a week between treatments.

MOON ENERGY, SUN ENERGY

The moon symbolizes feminine energy in many cultures around the world. To many Native Americans, the moon is the female Great Spirit, and the moon's influences represent female concerns and attributes. The menses are in many languages, including some European, called "moon," and many Native American women still refer to their menstrual time as "being on their moon."

On Earth, the moon controls the tides. If the moon can lift trillions of tons of water from the mighty ocean, do you suppose that it could have an effect on the pounds of water that make up a large percentage of your body? *The Farmer's Almanac* publishes detailed accounts of the moon's cycles because of their effects on the growth of crops and many people plan activities to coincide with phases of the moon.

The feminine aspect of humans is the intuitive, emotional, creative, receiving, empathic, and loving nature. Native American philosophy, like other great religions of the world, stressed the importance of the duality of human nature and the growth toward balance as a way of raising one's spiritual nature. There is negative-positive, man-woman, day-night, good-bad, and love-hate. It is desirable to achieve both emotional (feminine) and mental (masculine) qualities. One needs both right brain and left brain functioning. The special dominance of each need waxes and wanes to coincide with cyclic events in life.

In mythology, the waxing moon represents new life, beginnings, youth, innocence, creation, growth experimentation, and the prepubescent female. The full moon represents sex, fertility, power, fruition, harvest, maturity, completion, and woman. The waning moon signifies endings, death, disintegration, wisdom, evolution, transformation, destruction or reorder, and the old woman.

In astrology, the moon represents the feminine and feeling. Although most people are aware of their sun sign, many do not realize that they also have a moon sign (the zodiacal sign the moon was in at their birth). This

sign tells you how you handle your emotions and, in esoteric astrology, gives you information about past lives.

No Native American tribe identified the moon (Mother Moon) as masculine although several viewed the sun (Father Sun to most) as feminine. The impact of the aspects of our feminine nature, such as our right brains, is important for men as well as women. Just as full moon ceremonies have healing qualities for the female organs, they are equally soothing and balancing to male bodies as well. They are especially beneficial for those persons who wish to increase their sensitivity and creativity.

◧ FULL MOON CEREMONY

This ceremony can be performed only by women or by a mixed group of women and men. If women alone are present, a circle is formed. If men are also present, they form a ring around the women. (It is not necessary for the men to be close together, so only a few can occupy the outside circle.) Native American men did not attend activities inside the women's isolation hut, but did take part in the community ceremonies.

The moon ceremony can also be performed by one person if desired. There is no set number for optimum effects, although at least three women may be helpful to attract moon energy to the circle. The more positive people present, the more successful the ceremony. Negative or irreverent people will likely hinder results. It is important that the ritual not begin until all are seated in the circle. No one should break the circle or leave during the ceremony.

Ideally, the ritual should be performed as close to the height of the full moon as possible. An astrological calendar or almanac will provide this information. If the time is not practical, it can be done one day before or two days after the moon is at its fullest. During summer, it is best to perform the ceremony out-of-doors, because this will give it a special feeling. However, the moon has no trouble sending her special powers into your home or building.

One woman should be designated to read the following suggested

script. You can make additions in order to further personalize the directions. *Each sentence is to be read slowly. Pause between sentences.* Choose a person with a low, melodious voice, if possible. Celestial music, tinkling chimes, or soothing Native American chanting will also enhance the results.

This ceremony was given to Sunne Nelson, a psychic with sight into the fourth dimension, by her Indian spirit guide, Shaw Tah Wah Nee. The ceremony should be performed sitting comfortably, with legs crossed or straight. Relax as much as possible. Then slowly, read the script as follows:

Imagine the moon above your head shining down into your head where your hair naturally parts. Visualize the moon about six inches above your head. Feel how bright and heavy it is.

See an elixir drip from the moon. Feel it slide slowly into the crown of your head.

(Pause)

Feel the elixir trickling down into your throat, down into your chest cavity, and into your stomach. Now feel it dripping down into your pelvic area. Breathe it, feel it, know it is there. See the elixir moving down your thighs and toward your kneecaps, down to your lower legs, and toward your feet. As it begins to drip out of your body into the circle, you will feel as though you are sitting in this elixir.

(Silence for six or seven minutes)

See it filling up the circle. We are all sitting in this elixir and everyone's body is glowing with this beautiful light.

(Pause)

Beloved father, mother, god, bring the light shining forth to each and every person (woman/man) in the circle. Thy cup runneth over and I have spoken in your name.

Now, I want you to begin to breathe slowly and deeply. Take very even breaths. Raise your arms up toward the moon with palms facing outward. Reach for the moon. Call forth its energy to come into your body.

Give thanks in each and every way for the light that the moon gives us. Now bring your hands down on your knees and rest them there. Now I want you to visualize the moon beaming down this elixir in energy form, in little sparkles, and bring it into the center of your palms. As you breathe in, breathe in the energy from the moon, and when you breathe out, feel the energy still coming into the palms of your hands.

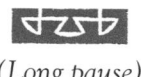

(Long pause)

Take your left hand and place it on top of your head, palm down; place your right hand, palm toward you, on your third eye, which is between your eyes in the center of your forehead. Breathe in, and as you breathe out, allow the energy from your hands to be released from your hands into your head area.

You are now going to bathe your chakras with the white light of the moon. Breathe in and breathe out, cleaning and clearing away all the debris, all the mental anguish and distress, filling your beautiful head with beautiful light.

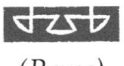

(Pause)

Take your left hand from the top of your head and place it on your throat, leave the right hand on your forehead, bathe your throat with this energy, breathe in deeply and breathe out, letting the air come slowly out of your mouth.

(Pause)

Now, I want you to take your right hand and gently place it on your heart. Leave your left hand on your throat. Blow all negativity out of your body, breathe in light, breathe out with a slight noise through your mouth. Let go. Let go. Let go. Breathe out again. Now, move your left hand from your throat, down over the stomach, leaving the right hand on the heart. Breathe in elixir, breathe out stress.

(Pause)

Relax your shoulders, leaving the hands on the body, relax those stom-ach muscles. Take your right hand from your heart and move it near your pelvic region (women—cover your ovaries and uterus). I want you to rock forward just a little bit, moving, swaying, gently, back and forth, just a little bit, back and forth rocking, breathing in energy and relieving stress in that part of your body.

You probably will notice where your body holds most of its tension while you are doing this—maybe in your back or shoulders. Let those areas relax. You should begin to feel a little heat going into your hand from your solar plexus. You will notice a little difference in the way it feels.

Now take your left hand from your stomach and put it right under the tip of your spine (your tail bone) under where you sit. Cup it there, breathe, and let go, breathe and let go. Feel the pulsations on your left hand as the energy goes through your body.

(Pause)

Now, let your hands drop down to your sides and relax.

Breathe and let the air out through your nose. Hold your hands up so that the energy flows up toward the sky. Your hands will feel peculiar from all the energy. Your hands will be pulsating. This is the energy you have taken away from your body that did not need to be there. Imagine this unwanted energy leaving your body and disappearing into space. All the undesirable vibrations have left your body. Keep sending it upward. The marvelous light from the moon has restored your natural vitality.

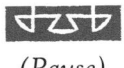

(Pause)

Place your hands on the floor, palms down on the sides of your body. Get in touch with the earth's vibrations. Imagine that you have a golden rod coming down through your spine, running straight down into the earth, until it hits the center of the earth. Only you can tell when this is. Sit in the silence and you will begin to feel the earth move. You will begin to feel the vibration of the earth through your palms on the ground (floor). You now have aligned your chakras through the earth and you will feel the earth's energy in your hands. Breathe gently. I will be quiet now while you absorb the earth's energy.

(Silence for six or seven minutes)

Now put both of your hands on your chest, palms toward your body. Seep the energy into your chest, breathe it in, put some emotion into it, breathe the energy into the chest. Now everyone in the circle join hands. Ask the Indian woman spirits to join our circle. Ask them any way you like. Everyone now ask for an Indian spirit to come into your life, to help you, guide you, and direct you in the areas that promote healing and cleansing within your own sphere and family. Ask it to stay with you for at least a month to help you and guide you.

Now begin to see white light come out of your forehead into the center of the circle. Imagine it. See Mother Earth in the center of our circle with Mother Moon above her giving energy into the earth. Ask that all the people—men, women, male children, female children—be cleansed and affected spiritually, whether they be our new leaders or whether they need to learn about love and emotion. See energy radiating from all the women's bodies on earth, being sent out to all men on the earth. Feel them rejoicing in femininity and love.

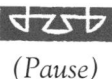

(Pause)

Give thanks to all the things you would like to give thanks for. Thank you, beloved father, mother, god.

◨ FULL MOON COMMUNICATION

This exercise may be done alone or with a close friend. Sit outside under a tree or around vegetation. If it is too cold, sit inside where you can see the moon. Stare at the moon in silence. Take time to reflect on the beauty of the moonlight and on the wonder of nature around you. Be appreciative of your life and of the marvelous light and the influence of the moon. Feel the power of the moon coming down into the top of your head. Enjoy the energy for at least ten to fifteen minutes.

Acknowledge the Moon Mother as an enormously powerful feminine entity. Begin to see her face. You may notice that her mouth seems to be open to answer your question or to give you advice. She specializes in affairs of the heart, feelings, creativity, spontaneity, and psychic abilities. Ask her for answers. Feel her light and warmth and watch her mouth move. Hear the answers she gives to you.

◧ Morning Sun Chant

In the morning, take your drum or rattle and go outside and face the sun. Feel the warmth on your face. Do not look directly into the sun, but sweep your eyes under the sun for four or seven times. This allows the energy from Father Sun to revitalize your body through your pituitary gland.

Beat your drum or use your rattle or hands to reach up to the sun like a bird in flight. Feel the reverence for the Sun Being that gives you light and life. Let the rays of the sun come through your palms and into your body. While using your instrument or moving your hands, begin to chant whatever comes to your mind. Do not analyze the sounds or words, just let them flow. You are giving thanks to the Sun Being, and he will give you a song or chant for your use. Let it happen.

Most Native American prayers and chants were quite simple and repetitious. They often repeat phrases four or seven times during ceremonies. For example, a simple chant to the Sun Being might be: "Great Morning, Sun Spirit. See me here below. Give me power. See me here below. Take my pain. See me here below. Hear my plea. See me here below." Put a simple melody to the words and you have a powerful prayer.

◧ Setting Sun Chant

The setting sun provides another opportunity for prayer and song: "Setting Sun Spirit. Lay me down with peace. Take my enemies. Lay me down with peace. Give me rest. Lay me down with peace. A (man/woman) asks for you. Lay me down with peace."

APPENDICIES

APPENDIX A

Notes

1 (*page 10*) Dr. Benjamin Barton, "Collections for an Essay Towards Materia Medicaof the United States," as researched by Virgil J. Vogel, *American Indian Medicine*, University of Oklahoma Press, 1970

2 (*page 10*) John Lawson, *A New Voyage to South Carolina*, Chapel Hill, 1967

3 (*page 39*) Bird and animal interpretation in *Native American Magic and Medicine* by Mary Atwood, Sterling Publishing Co., Inc., NY 1991

4 (*page 49*) Richard Lucas, *Common & Uncommon uses of Herbs for Healthful Living*, Arco, 1982

5 (*page 50*) Mary Atwood, *Native American Magic and Medicine*, Sterling Publishing Co., Inc., NY 1991 (describes how to do a vision quest)

6 (*page 59*) Virgil J. Vogel, *American Indian Medicine*, University of Oklahoma Press,1970

7 (*page 60*) Ibid

8 (*page 82*) Harold Driver, *Indians of North America*, University of Chicago Press, 1961

9 (*page 82*) Ibid

10 (*page 82*) Ibid

11 (*page 82*) Michael Weiner, *Earth Medicine Earth Food*, Ballantine Books, 1972

12 (*page 83*) John Heinerman, author of *Science of Herbal Medicine*, BiWorld Publishers: Orem, Utah, 1984

13 (*page 83*) Ibid

14 (*page 84*) Vaughn M. Bryant, Jr., "The Role of Coprolite Analysis in Archeology;" Bulletin of the Texas Archaeological Society, Vol. 45, 1974

15 (*page 86*) Jon Manchip White, *Everyday Life of the North American Indian*, Dorsett Press, NY 1979

16 (*page 86*) Gene Weltfish, *The Lost Universe: Pawnee Life and Culture*, Nebraska Press, 1977

17 (*page 103*) Small section of the vision by Black Elk in 1932 written in *Black Elk Speaks* by John Neihardt

18 (*page 106*) John Heinerman, author of *Science of Herbal Medicine*, BiWorld Publishers: Orem, Utah, 1984

19 (*page 115*) Humbert Santillo, N.D. author of *Natural Healing with Herbs*, Hohm Press, Prescott, AZ 1993

20 (*page 116*) Paul B. Hamel & Mary U. Chiltoskey, *Cherokee Plants, their uses—a 400 year history.* Library of Congress Catalog Card Number 75-27776

21 (*page 116*) Melvin Gilmore, *Uses of Plants by the Indians of the Missouri River Region*, University of Nebraska Press, 1977

22 (*page 117*) Alma Hutchens, *Indian Herbalogy of North America*, Shambhala, Boston, 1973

23 (*page 133*) Harold Driver, *Indians of North America*, University of Chicago Press, 1961

24 (*page 134*) Jack Henningfield of the National Institute of Drug Abuse in *Brain/Mind Bulletin*, 1986

25 (*page 138*) *Journal of a Voyage to North America*, Ed. Louise Phelps Kellogg, reported by Virgil Vogel in *American Indian Medicine*

26 (*page 139*) Joseph Epes Brown is interpreting the meaning of terms used by the White Buffalo Maiden told to him by Black Elk and written in Brown's book *The Sacred Pipe*, University of Oklahoma Press, 1953

27 (*page 142*) A Lakota Indian quoted in *Pipe, Bible and Peyote Among the Oglala Lakota*, by Stein, Metz, and Alquist, Stockholm

28 (*page 142*) Joseph Epes Brown is interpreting the meaning of terms used by the White Buffalo Maiden told to him by Black Elk and written in Brown's book *The Sacred Pipe*, University of Oklahoma Press, 1953

29 (*page 143*) Translated by Paul Radin, in "Autobiography of Winnebago Indian," University of California Publications in *American Archeology and Ethnology*, Vol. 17, #7, 1920

Appendix B

Color Visualization Analysis

Use this as a measure of progress and verification of spiritual levels. At this point, do not worry about achieving the color purple in your mind's eye; it will appear later.

Purple

Crown energy center and the desired color for communication with the highest spirit guides. The goal is to perceive a purple color in your mind's eye. The purple is a signal you are at a high enough vibratory level (spiritually speaking) to be able to communicate with your spirit helpers. For most people it is necessary to practice before they can envision purplish hues.

Indigo (dark, red-tinted blue)

The third eye energy center, through which you may intuit messages from your guides, or at least your higher self. Those seeing blue, indigo, or similar shades find they soon can raise the level to purple during meditation, with practice.

Blue

Throat energy center used to receive messages from your self or higher self. This is the location of the mental/energy center where thoughts originate. Some people start out in the blue and then raise their color level during their spiritual conference.

Yellow

Heart energy center where higher feelings such as love and devotion originate. Attachments, attractions, and yearnings also derive from this center. People seeing yellow are on a higher emotional plane but must raise their consciousness to a mental/spiritual level for communication with their guides or higher self. It is fairly easy for those individuals on this level to begin to see blue or purple.

Green

Solar plexus center is a person's power base. Here the personality exerts will and self-control. Emotion often rules. Fear, jealousy, and anger originate from this center. A predominant green color may indicate either an obsession with loss of control or fear. If you see this color, then emotional concerns of every-day living are interfering with your higher spiritual development and communication. One of the most common reasons for this is that you were not in a relaxed enough state when you started.

Red or Orange Red

Root center operating on a physical level, concerned with basic safety and physiological needs. People who continue to see only red or orange after repeated practice will need other measures to achieve the higher colors. Prayer, meditation, reading of spiritual literature, or change in routine is sometimes necessary. Sometimes it helps to ponder current security fears or passions that tend to keep the individual at the root level. Patience and practice may be required to shift the consciousness toward higher levels.

Black

Occasionally, a person will see black. This may mean a problem with visualizing, which can be helped by trying to smell, feel, or taste the color purple. Sometimes black means that a person is ready to drop off to sleep. If you are one of those people who go to sleep instantly when you go to bed, you should meditate upright in a sitting position.

INDEX